JOURNEY OUT OF ASIA

JOURNEY OUT OF ASIA

by

KATHARINE SIM

Illustrated

ROBERT HALE LIMITED

© Katharine Sim 1963

First published
in Great Britain 1963
by Robert Hale Limited
63 Old Brompton Road
London S.W.7
and printed by
Willmer Brothers
& Haram Limited
Birkenhead

For our sons
JONATHAN
and
ANDREW

'Biar rentang, jangan putus'
'Let it be stretched, but not broken'
Malay proverb

This is the story of a journey of
of 12,500 miles across Asia and into
Europe, made not only for the experience and pleasure of it, but in
the hope that the thread of our
love for the East and for Malaya in
particular might be stretched, not
broken off abruptly, before we
started a new life in England.

CONTENTS

ILLUSTRATIONS

JOURNEY OUT OF
ASIA

The route: by road ↓↓↓↓
by air ← ← ← ← , by sea ~~~~
scale, approx. 350 miles = 1"

Katharine Sim. 1961.

inset map
scale approx.
150 ms. = 1"

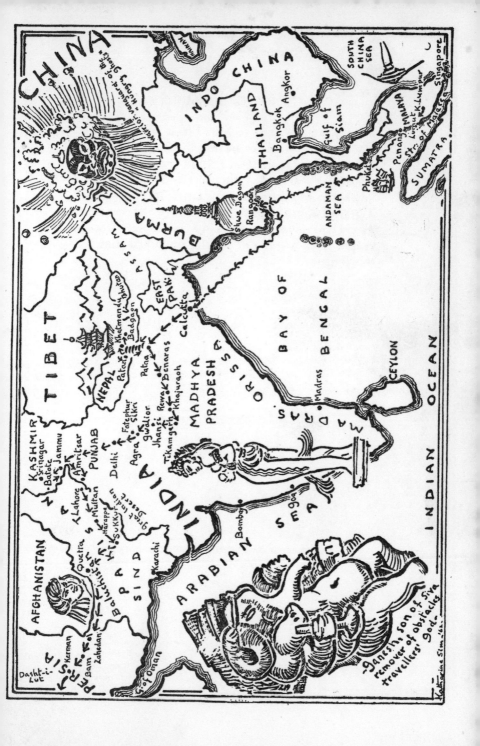

CHINA

INDO CHINA

THAILAND

Bangkok Angkor

SOUTH CHINA SEA

MALAYA   Singapore

Penang Str. of Malacca K. Lumpur

SUMATRA

Gulf of Siam

Phuket

BURMA

Shwe Dagon Rangoon

ANDAMAN SEA

ASSAM

TIBET

KASHMIR
Srinagar
Baltals Jammu

NEPAL
Khatmandu Bhutan
Patna Badgaon
Patna

EAST PAK.

Calcutta

BAY OF BENGAL

MADHYA PRADESH

ORISSA

CEYLON

INDIAN OCEAN

PUNJAB
Amritsar
Lahore Delhi
Multan Fatephur Sikri
Agra Gwalior
Jhansi Tikamgerh Rewa Benaras
Khajuraoh

MADRAS

Madras

AFGHANISTAN

Quetta
Baluchistan
Harappa
Sukkur SIND
Karachi

INDIA

Great Indian Desert

Bombay

Goa

ARABIAN SEA

PERSIA
Kerman
Dasht-i-Lut Bam
Zahedan

Ganesh, son of Siva
remover of obstacles, God
travellers' God.

ACKNOWLEDGEMENTS

My sincere gratitude to Miss Freya Stark, and to Mr W. D. P. Hill for having so kindly read the M.S., and for their most helpful comments. And my thanks also to the Editor of *The Times* for permission to reprint part of an article on the White Tigers of Rewa, and to the Editor of the *Sunday Times* (Malaya) for allowing me to use paragraphs from a series of articles published during this journey.

K. S.

❧ 1 ❧

Days out of Time in Malaya

Farewells had been said: doors shut, we were ready to go: two people had followed us down to the van, and now through the open window each in silence gripped my hands in one of theirs— brown and ivory, Malay and Chinese.

I managed to hold back my tears then. Stuart let in the clutch, camera shutters clicked, the little group of people under the hotel porch drew back and stood waving as the van moved slowly away.

Then the tears stung and blinded: I hardly saw the familiar streets of Kuala Lumpur, leaving them finally that Sunday morning in January 1960 on the first lap of our long journey home to England.

It was early, and the sun was shining softly. For us it was a great adventure that lay ahead; months in fresh lands—new experiences, unknown hazards—I should have been happy, but for a while I could only weep. It had not been easy to say goodbye to well-loved people whom one could not expect to see again; nor was it going to be easy to leave a country that in over twenty years had become infinitely more than a second home to my husband and to me.

The Malays say that the thread of love should never be broken suddenly: '*biar rentang, jangan putus*'—let it be stretched, not snapped. Stuart and I both loved Malaya too well to leave it suddenly by the normal ways of sea or air. So, months previously we had decided that, when the time came, we would travel home overland by car.

Once well clear of the town, Stuart drew into the side of the road near an old mining pool, switched off the engine, and grinned at me. I blew my nose and tried to dry my tears.

'Sorry!' I mumbled, knowing I must look both horrible and depressing.

'Never mind. Have a good weep!' he said gently.

He jumped out, went to the side doors of the van, and poured two short brandies. I felt considerably better after that, and then I climbed into the back to rest. I did not really want to see the road, the hills, the camphor forest, the turning to the East Coast, nor the deep-chested white egrets—all these things were at that moment painful symbols of the Malaya I loved, and must leave.

The last few months in Kuala Lumpur had been both hard working and madly gay; crammed with ideas and plans; happy, and sad too.

I lay thinking of it all, as Stuart drove northwards. The little van purred noisily as if glad to be on the road again. I'd always felt that the van had a personality, like an animate being; it was not just a car to us, it was a home, even a vessel, in fact we'd named it the Ark, and it was to become more to us in the months ahead than many a house we had lived in.

A considerable amount of planning had gone into this venture. In the summer of 1959 we had bought the van, a Volkswagen-Kombi; and with the aid of the local agents we converted it, strengthened it in various ways and made it suitable for a long journey. I looked around me now with pleasure : the light grey-green interior was cool and restful to the eyes. The chrome yellow curtains and cushion covers, which we had chosen together, were exactly right, durable and yet gay. The silky covers of the foam rubber mattresses were soft and pleasant to feel. The roof was insulated with fibre glass, and its neatly ribbed finish, a craftsman-like job, reminded one of an air-liner. The cupboards for reference books and for clothes were now filled; my drawing-board and folio stowed in a slot behind the bulkhead of the driving cab; the sturdy folding table in place alongside the bed; numerous fitted boxes under the bed were well stocked with stores and gear—and Ararat, the toy terrier given to us by some Polish friends as a mascot, stood by one window.

I turned my head so that I could see the 'pin-ups' of our sons, their bright eyes and smiling young faces cheered me. I told myself that I would surely stop thinking about Malaya one day. The future was, after all, ahead with them in England. Stuart was retiring from Malayan Government Service two years before he needed to after Independence, largely for their sakes, primarily because we both believed that an English education is still the best in the world.

But change does not come easily in the forties, after years of congenial work in the tropical land of one's adoption; I thought again of that saying : '*biar rentang, jangan putus*'. And now here we were, at the very start of our journey, determined to stretch that thread slowly. Slowly to ease the bonds that held us both so strongly to Malaya through loving familiarity with her shores, hills and islands.

I sat up, and pulled the curtains apart. In the dazzling sunshine the light-coloured, green-fringed Malayan road slipped away behind, as if it were going south, and only we were pressing on to the north. Now our direction would nearly always lie to the north-west; away from the sun, away from the east. The first stretching of the cord had begun.

Stuart slowed down as we approached a little town; it was midday, and a wonderful smell of spicy foods cooking filled the air—Malay, Indian and Chinese, and I suddenly felt intensely hungry as if I'd not eaten for days; tears and emotion invariably having this odd effect on me.

I crouched up on the pillows to speak to Stuart through the space behind the driving seat at the head of the bed. He brought the van to a stop, and I climbed into the front seat beside him for company.

It was pleasant driving in Ark; the high seat afforded a clear view of the road, and it was always cool even in the tropics.

We began to talk about Lumut, our destination that day, and of the immediate future. Having some time ago abandoned the idea of attempting the difficult roads of Burma without a four-wheel drive (as it transpired ultimately we could not have obtained visas to do so at that time), we had arranged to ship the van from Penang to Calcutta. But the shipping schedule had recently been altered, so that we now had about three weeks in hand. Stuart had planned a farewell visit to Lumut and the Sembilan Islands on our way north, and the rest of the time we would spend in South Siam and, lastly, in Penang, preparing Ark and ourselves for the short sea voyage to India.

Lumut was a place of many and varied memories. We had lived there from 1939 until the Japanese invasion in 1941, and experienced both extreme happiness, and great distress. There was the war in Europe, and ultimately the bitterness of forced parting at the time of the invasion, the loss of our home, the shame and wretchedness of leaving our Chinese servants. And on the other hand there was the happiness of youth, of love and sunshine, and my first taste of Malaya's dream-like islands.

We fell silent again; we did not talk much that day, both being tired out with emotion and lack of sleep. When we had eaten by the roadside, Stuart took his turn to rest in the back while I drove —on past the limestone hills of Perak, and westwards down the long road towards the coast.

We had been married nearly twenty-two years, and naturally enough I began to think of the times in Lumut, and out at the islands, when we had been young and relatively irresponsible.

At Lumut, the launch was waiting; the crew welcomed us with smiles, some of them whom we knew well, with that gentle understanding that Malays particularly seem able to express through look or manner, without speaking. I was perfectly well aware that they knew what we were feeling about leaving their country. They put long chairs for us on the stern, and we lay there, limp, utterly exhausted as the launch put out to sea. The sun was setting over Pangkor Island and the tall hilly outlines of the Dindings coast beyond as we drew near to the Sembilan Islands; then clouds swept up from the east. Presently Stuart slept, and I wished I could also, but I was too sad still for sleep.

Because of the freshening sunset wind it was rough off the point at Rumbia as we came round to the anchorage in the little bay. Four great sea eagles were swooping over the hill, calling and calling harshly in the brief dusk. It was always a difficult anchorage because of the tides off that point and the under-water coral in the bay. But at last we were safely anchored, and soon large plates of hot rice, kampong style very hotly curried fish and aubergine revived us both. Then we put up our camp beds on the stern, and for a little while watched the phosphorescence floating past on the tide, bright but not glittering globules of light, like small lamps; then we slept deeply, until dawn rocked on the gentle swell in the bay.

The morning was perfect, the clouds gone. The fourteen leaning palms stood over the white sands just as I remembered them from my initial visits, when Rumbia was the first of my desert island dreams to materialize. Since then, and particularly in the last five or six years, I had seen even more beautiful, wilder islands; those of Trengganu and Kelantan, ringed with white and with circles of ever-deepening blue in the miraculous clarity of the

South China Sea. There we had swum daylong over the coral, and with our sons had dived for the shining porcelain contours of tiger cowries half-veiled in living mantles, and for the exquisite, rosy-clawed shapes of scorpion shells.

The West Coast sea, the Malacca Straits, has not this remarkable turquoise clarity, it is more of an emerald green near the islands, and rarely clear off the coast. But nevertheless I had a very warm spot in my heart for little jungly Rumbia, with its saddle-back headland and emerald bay. The bay now was dark where coral showed beneath it, and blue with the blue of the sky in the gentle lift and flow and movement of the ebbing tide.

Some fishermen came in to salt their catch in ragged huts under the tall jungle by a spring in the corner of the bay. So we went ashore to buy a few of their fresh fish and some ice, while the men fetched water from the spring.

The big old *kêtapang* tree still threw its shade across the sand, its leaves red at this season, almost trailing in the sea. I swam back lazily to the launch, and watched Stuart, who is a keen conchologist, searching at the far end of the bay for shells among the sea-wrack there. As I sat drying in the sun, a good clean smell of rice cooking came up from the galley, bringing with it a sharp evocation of ripe grain in the husk, and of all the harvests I had seen in Malacca; men and women working in the golden fields, the blue cone of Mount Ophir with her small white scarf of cloud—Shimmering Mountain of the legends . . .

I watched the men working on the beach in the shade of the big *Kêtapang* tree. A tiny curl of smoke from incense on the sea spirit rock nearby drifted up and was lost against the mass of dark foliage above. The sea eagles were quiet now, perhaps they were fishing. But I never knew any other island as raucous with cicadas as Rumbia. Their shrill sound rang out, in their accumulative whirring as loud as electric bells from the high jungle. Like a song to the sun, it seemed part of the heat, and of the vivid day.

Stuart had ceased to look for shells, and was swimming out leisurely now to the launch.

A sharp rich smell of fresh coconut oil hot in the pan followed that of the rice cooking, they would be preparing the chillies and and aubergine now. It's better than many a sophisticated dish, I thought—this kind of kampong meal eaten at sea, or in the villages.

There was always an angry race of waves off this easterly point

B

of Rumbia, where once, years ago, I had watched the first turtles I had ever seen, mating in the surging water, and a giant ray leaping clear beyond them. There was no sign of turtles now, and the bay was calm. This was peace indeed after all we had been through in the last few days and weeks—the rush, the tension, and the painfulness of parting with well-loved people. The gay parties, the formal ones, the kindness of all those who had tried to alleviate the sadness of departure : I felt the strain of it all begin to slough off me. This was balm.

The crew, moving quietly about their jobs, paused to talk, to ask after our sons then both at school in England. Their brown-gold Malay faces were smiling, their voices soft and kindly, again I was most conscious of unspoken sympathy.

Stuart climbed aboard, the drops sparkling off him in the hot sunshine. He stood drying himself lazily, the water falling from him soon darkened the white, sun-baked deck as if a little pool of shadow lay at his feet. But he had scarcely any real shadow, for it was noon and we were only five degrees north.

I could see that the tension was easing for him too. The healing sea, and the peace of the islands work quickly. The desert, as I came to know later, has this same power over the spirit, but in a very different way.

The tide was setting inshore now suddenly and with tremendous speed, as I could tell from the movement of the sea-wrack. A collection of seeds of all sorts, some already sprouting; water-logged sticks; a large dead king crab prehistoric-looking in his armour; twirling coconuts, and the usual escort of fish, a vanguard of smaller ones, *kembong* perhaps, and at a deeper level plump *bawal,* swimming sedately. Beautiful as the bay was, it had never been an easy anchorage; and now with this fast tide setting in, once again the anchor fouled the coral, and the chain ran out. So we moved around to Turtle Bay on the west side, there our *hors-d'oeuvres* was little oysters—the freshest I have ever tasted —sliced off the rocks with Stuart's underwater knife. After the swim we lunched on board off fresh *bawal* (a kind of prom-fret), salted fish and a curry so hot it almost burnt the lips but it was good in its own way after the sun and salt of the sea. After lunch we swam yet again, out over the reef this time, to see Neptune cups far below, a 'Moorish idol' or two, delicate and trim, an ugly old groper chasing a bevy of blue and gold coral fish.

Before sunset we swam for the last time at another island, Pulau Lallang. As it has no water, it is a real desert island, not even a passing fisherman puts in there. It must have always been so, pure and unspoilt, with its pigeons and eagles, wild fruit trees and undefiled white sands. I left it with a backward look of regret. Would I ever see such a place again; wild, beautiful, green, warm and pristine? It must be exactly as Lancaster saw it—when he passed down these Straits in 1791, and with his crew half starving raided a rich Portuguese trader at these very islands.

We anchored for the night off Pangkor Island. Our time at the islands was nearly over, and on the following morning we were to set off north again from Lumut.

It was a night of brilliant stars over the dark, sugar-cone hills of Pangkor, we sat and talked for a long time. All that I recall about it now was a sense of a quieter spirit, a well-sunned, and at last a rested body. And one odd little thing too: typical of the extraordinary phosphorescence of the Malacca Straits—when I opened the ice box in the dark, I saw that some fish which the men had put there lay gleaming like fire opals, X-rayed as if lit from within, every bone etched in light.

We sipped our stengahs and sat talking about the future, and as we had done a hundred times—of the places we most hoped to see—Khatmandu, Isfahan and, above all—Petra.

Stuart, ever more practical than I am, stressed how far south Petra lay in Jordan, and again warned me not to be too bitterly disappointed if we were unable to make the long diversion.

The Syrian part of the journey had meant obtaining no less than sixteen visas, for we had planned to rest twice in Beirut, where we had relatives. Therefore we needed eight visas each for Syrian frontiers which we would have to pass four times in and four times out. This had been one of our worst problems, and at that time, it was shortly after Suez, relations with the U.A.R. had scarcely been favourable. It had taken nearly seven months to acquire the visas in Kuala Lumpur from the Legation which, in the end, had proved friendly and helpful. So for a long while our hopes of seeing Petra had hung dangerously in the balance.

Since my early childhood I had dreamed of Petra: now sitting there on the launch under the stars above that quiet sea, it did seem more likely that we should reach it—somehow, at *some* time in the exciting months that lay ahead.

✱ 2 ✱

Penang to Calcutta

Those two nights and a day at the islands were hours stolen from time; but they had restored us both, and now we took to the road again with renewed heart and a growing sense of anticipation.

We hurried north through Perak, the State in which Stuart had commenced his Malayan career in 1934; up through Krian with a brief pause to call on the wife of our pre-war driver. She was out in the fields, harvesting the paddy, hot and dishevelled she welcomed us with apologies for her appearance. The entire family, she insisted, were coming up to Penang later, to bid us farewell in proper style.

Krian was looking beautiful as always, with its wide dykes, level fields, and great creeper-hung shade trees at the roadside. Penang Island loomed ahead, its long hill a soft familiar outline dark against the west; Kedah Peak a lovely jagged contrast stood to the north-east. Chinese junks lay clustered darkly in the strait against the warm south-west, the silvery Straits of Malacca.

It was the first day of Chinese New Year, in the Year of the Rat when we drove on towards Siam. I wished that we did not have to return to ship from Penang, I was not looking forward to a second dose of farewells, but the delay was inevitable now that the direct drive northwards through Burma was impossible. As it happened we gained some useful tips on the shocking roads of South Siam, for the roads of Malaya are excellent, and so far we had had no experience of the Ark's capabilities on really bad surfaces.

I think it was on the return journey from Siam, when we were once again on good Malayan roads and rapidly drawing near to Penang, that I counted up the ferries—five to cross on the trek to England. They would be, from the mainland of Malaya to Penang; from Asia into Europe at the Bosphorus; from Greece to Corfu; from Corfu to Brindisi; and lastly from Calais to Dover.

We crossed the first of those five ferries on leaving the Malayan mainland, late one afternoon in February. We were both silent, too well aware of what the other was thinking; this was goodbye to Malaya, the beloved country.

Mentally I squared my shoulders: the interlude in Siam had deepened our confidence for the trek, we now knew more of Ark's ability, of how we might better arrange our load, the necessity of a second set of horns, and—to our cost—where dust penetrated most. It had also provided something on which to dwell, other than this painfully protracted series of farewells.

Penang: I had first seen it early one morning in 1938 as the P. and O. liner swept in around the north head.

I had gone out to Malaya all those years ago because I loved my husband, but I had believed that I was leaving the best of civilization behind. It did not take me long to revise my ideas and in a few months' time I was deeply in love with the country. Malaya gave me, over the years, countless opportunities for work and joy, and unforgettable riches not of worldly wealth.

The ferry moved briskly across the two and a quarter mile strait. The long hump-backed shape of Penang Island drew rapidly nearer; the noise of the engines and of the waves was loud in our ears, the spray and the tangy scent of the sea clean in our nostrils.

I'd always loved Penang harbour, with its ships, sampans, junks and launches, its Italianate water-front, and its tall clock tower at the station without any trains. As the ferry drew closer I could see far away in the hills beyond the town the white pagoda of the Monastery of Supreme Content—the Kek Lok Si. I thought of our good friend Wong* and of how we had explored with him many of the one hundred and twenty or so island temples, learning their cults and secrets, and with his aid translating their often beautiful names into English—Heavenly Dragons, Jade Emperor, Sea Pearl Monastery, Purple Bamboo Grove, Compassionate Navigation . . .

The engine-room bell rang shrilly, the ferry slowed down and nosed her way into the landing-stage berth. Ramps were lowered, and then, quickly—with fish lorries, cars, jeeps and motor-cycles, we drove ashore, and through the town. A few minutes later we arrived at a house in Scotland Road where we were to stay for a week with our friend, Selwyn Buckwell, until the ship sailed. It

* C. S. Wong of Penang.

was a moot point as to whether he could endure us that long; he is an old and well-loved friend, but he has always said that 'the Sims' revolting energy' exhausts him in two days. However, somehow or other he survived that week, and during it he was as usual a most amusing companion to us both and a stalwart support, for we had, as he put it himself, been brother, sister and brother for a great many years. In the end I think we all wore each other out talking until the small hours, and enjoying our last days in Penang to the utmost.

There was a large amount of mail awaiting us including a rather touching farewell song written in Malay. We learnt that Lady Louis,* then on a St John's tour, was leaving Penang the following day, and she sent a message asking us to meet her at the Governor's house that evening.

It was ten-thirty after an official dinner, and the Governor and his lady had already gone to bed, so our last meeting with Lady Louis was pleasantly quiet and informal. With her usual lively interest and range of sympathy she asked questions about our plans; when we mentioned Petra, she was enthusiastic, she herself had visited it no less than three times. I thought this was typical of Lady Louis—of her energy, vitality and enterprise.

'It is one of *the* unforgettable wonders of the world,' she said.

When it was time for us to go she came out into the garden to see Ark.

'It looks like some kind of prehistoric animal!' she laughed, '—with those great eyes.'

I had often thought so myself; Ark's headlamps do look like eyes that appear to be glancing perhaps a little askance in a flattened face.

She kissed me goodbye; then suddenly, to my great delight said that she would ask the U.K. Consul in New Delhi to look out for us and to try to arrange for a meeting with Mr Nehru. She had been staying with Nehru in New Delhi, and she knew one of my ambitions was to meet him.

Early the next morning Stuart and I drove down to Penang's little airport in the south of the island to see her off. We watched her in her dark St John's uniform, waving her white gloved hand and we did not think then that this was a final goodbye.

The week sped by. It had taken a long time to clean the red

* The Countess Mountbatten of Burma.

Siamese dust out of the Ark, and I had spent a few rather unpleasant hours chewing gum to fill some of the crevices in the
various rear cupboards where the dust flew in so thickly. It may
sound comic and I certainly received no sympathy as I sat there
champing away ridiculously; it was a jaw-aching task, but one
that did help a little in the deserts later.

The Malays from Krian came to pay their farewell visit, they
were loaded with large and elaborately-made presents. There were
visits from English and Chinese friends too, dinner parties, and a
final party at Selwyn's house. Throughout the week the island was
alive with colour and movement, for it so happened that there
were two festivals running concurrently, the Indian Thaipusam,
and the fifteenth day of the first Chinese moon. The brilliant
moonlight nights, so typical of Malaya—the palms shining as if
lacquered black and silver in the flooding radiance were all too
disturbingly beautiful. But with Selwyn's help we got through the
last days well, though I was glad in a sense when February the
fifteenth came, and it was time to go aboard the *s.s. Sirdhana*.
Unfortunately she was not alongside, but lying out in the roads.
With every good intention the Customs Department commanded
a launch to take us off; this was nearly my undoing. The launch
was shining and immaculate, the crew had put on their best
'whites'; their brown Malay faces, their dark brown eyes were
only too expressive, indeed several of those whom we knew well
looked as if they themselves were on the verge of breaking down
as we said goodbye. It was only a brief trip, and I was thankful to
be on board. I rushed to our cabin where Selwyn, patient and
long-suffering, tried to console me while Stuart coped on deck. But
sympathy, of course, is weakening, and again I had to weep. 'It's
a good thing,' he said. 'Tears are healing—it wouldn't be natural
if you didn't cry after all these years.'

I suppose he was right, but all I knew was utter thankfulness
that this was the last of these farewells.

Selwyn and a few other friends stayed on board and fortified us
with stengahs and talk until the ship was ready to sail. There was
the screech of the cable coming in, and then she crept away without a sound other than the steady hum of the dynamos, and the
peeping noise of the radar. Stuart and I stood up in the bows with
the deck passengers then, and watched the floodlit E. and O.
Hotel and the glow of the town slide by.

We stayed on deck for a long time watching the island slowly fading away astern under the light of the waning moon. The lights of the hill-top houses were like pointed stars, and those of the familiar places along the north coast evoked clear pictures in my mind of the past week; the gaiety of the Full Moon night, and the Fire Receiving ceremony at the Sea Pearl Monastery, the lighted joss sticks flung into the sea, and the boisterous waves of a high tide leaping like live things, as if acknowledging the prayers of the people. Gay young Chinese men dining ankle-deep in crab shells, enjoying a night out. . . . A last drive through the little green 'Vale of Tempe,' and to the Monastery of Supreme Content on a brilliant Sunday morning; streams of brightly-dressed worshippers, and after the joss and the prayers, bowls of chillie-hot *laksa* at the hill's foot. . . . Thaipusam too, with all its Indian colour and fervour; the joyous smashing of coconuts so that the roads ran with juice before the jewelled chariot towering, glittering behind its placid, dark-eyed bulls, drawing the god slowly on through the night, with music and lanterns, and little boys dancing backwards before him. . . .

Feeling rather like a ghost I crept out on deck late next morning, and saw the Siamese island of Phuket lying to the east, blue and pointed. It seemed odd to be back so close and so soon, after our recent long trundle down the cobbled roads of Siam. It was a glorious breezy day; gay little Gurkha girls, soldiers' daughters with red ribbons in their plaits and gold in their nostrils, were dancing about on the after-hatch. Their stalwart fathers and brothers sat cross-legged in orderly groups, gambling almost ceaselessly. The deck passengers were a vivid bunch, and for me their presence much enlivened the short voyage. I admired the manner in which they organized themselves and conducted their daily routine, shaving, eating, sleeping, playing, reading, all in public, with complete *savoir faire*.

Among the first-class passengers was a charming couple from Darjeeling, with the attractive name of Tenduf la—pronounced Tender Flower. The wife was a Tibetan from Lashio, gay and robust, with a clear complexion and intensely bright black eyes. She wore long sleeveless gowns of various colours over silk blouses; and always a heavy woven and embroidered apron, part of the traditional dress of Tibet. There was a shy Nepalese couple—the hus-

band was a guru—and their family of little boys, the eldest of
whom was beautiful, with widely-spaced light brown eyes in a
dreamy, waxen, petal-dark face. There was also a couple of
friendly Australians on a long tour—Roma and Phil Ford. Roma
was one of those fortunate women who always look the same, perhaps because of some inner radiance, a big, slim smiling girl with
a sparkling look. After a visit to Darjeeling and Southern India,
they had arranged to travel to England on the Bombay-London
bus—'the Indiaman'.

'Our friends say we're mad to go by bus!' Roma laughed, the
corners of her blue eyes crinkling.

'Some of ours think we're mad too—to drive home,' I said.

Phil brought out his notes on their schedule, and the bus
itinerary. We compared dates, and Stuart made a prophecy : 'I
should think we'll meet in Isfahan!'

It was a remarkably good guess as it so happened, but it did not
seem a very likely chance at the time. However, we arranged to
look out for each other and to leave a message whoever was first
through, at the Persian or Pakistan frontier.

We sailed up the Rangoon River at dawn followed by a host of
gulls, the first I had seen since leaving England eighteen months
before, they are not found as far south as Malaya. The great Shwe
Dagon shone above the town and the drab wharves, a softly
golden glory, luminous against the warm, grey-blue sky. The
pagoda is 368 feet high, a little higher than St Paul's. It is the
most venerable of all Buddhist places of worship in South-East
Asia because it is the one pagoda believed to contain not only
relics of Gautama himself but of the three Buddhas who preceded
him in this world. Part of it dates from 588 B.C.; today it remains
unaltered since A.D. 1564.

We went ashore as soon as our papers were cleared, and called
first at the British Embassy, as we had an introduction from John
Slimming, the writer, to a man there. This young man suggested
that I should get in touch with the Indian Press Attaché in Rangoon, and invited us to lunch after we had been to the pagoda.

We spent the rest of the morning inside the Shwe Dagon. The
taxi dropped us at the main entrance, where enormous Walt
Disney-like stone lions guard the approach to the great flight of
covered steps. Taking off our shoes, as one must, we climbed this
long and extremely dirty stairway. It is wide and spacious with

many landings, and is lined with stalls and little workshops, mainly of the carvers of delicate ivories, and the sellers of flowers and offerings, roses, and glittering paper *hti*,* and bright fragile baubles. At the top of this dark stairway the first visual impact of the vast sunlit marble terrace is tremendous. As one emerges into the brilliant sunlight, the terrace sparkles with its mass of gold leaf, twinkling glass mosaic, and countless pagodas. It was all so vivid against the hot pearly grey sky that the sight of it took my breath away, and it was a second or two before I became aware that my now filthy bare feet were slowly toasting on the hot marble.

For some time we wandered around, gazing in awe and delight, and every now and again retreating to cool the soles of our feet in the shadows. At noon a great bell sounded : pigeons and myriads of crows flew up noisily over the hundreds of golden spires—a glittering cage that fences in the giant central dome. I sat down then on a big chest in the shade opposite the Buddhas, to rest my burning feet. The interiors of the little encircling shrines were painted blood red or emerald green like jewels; the four great chapels glittered with glass, gold leaf, *hti* and flowers. Worshippers moved round the terrace—Burmese girls, charming in muslin jackets and flowered longhis; men, women and children prostrated themselves before the shrines and the plump little white elephants that kneel so attractively between each one.

After the noon bell the temple grew quiet : there was little noise but the gurgling cooing sound of countless pigeons nesting in many crannies, and the endless cawing of innumerable crows. People were picnicking under the shade trees, reading and even sleeping in the shrines.

Then someone came to move me off the money chest. Perhaps the reason for this was a superstition common among Chinese actors that a woman sitting on a money chest brings ill luck. I should have remembered for I had learnt this backstage in Penang Cantonese operas. I went and sat humbly on the steps below. Now everyone seemed to have vanished or to be asleep, only the gods in bronze and alabaster sat silent, serene-faced among the winking mosaics and brilliant gold and sugar-white spires.

When we eventually returned to the ship it took me nearly half an hour to scrub my feet clean. It seems that, unlike Muslims,

* *Hti,* a kind of ceremonial umbrella, the uppermost top of a pagoda or an offering symbolic of this.

Buddhists at least in Burma, do not often wash their temple floors, but I felt that a few ounces of dirt mattered little when there was such a splendour of colour and light above the sun-baked marble.

By night the Shwe Dagon was even more impressive than by day, and the Fords joined us on a second visit which enchanted us all. To step out then from the cavern-dark well of the stairs onto that terrace was to walk into a fairy land, a lavish fantasy, and yet one that was real, solid, webbed with the atmosphere of centuries. The multitude of dark pagodas, each with its aspiring *hti*, rose dusky almost reddish—a forest of dragon's teeth against the shining, lighted gold sides of the central dome, and the blue moon-lit paleness of the sugar-white chapels. The dim, candle-lit interiors of the small shrines, where each quiet alabaster figure sat alone, now appeared in their varying, true subtle colours. It was peaceful; only the bells tinkled in the breeze, and only a few worshippers deep in silent prayer lingered in the chapels. Around these small bowed human figures there was an eternally winking, moving splendour of pillar and inner shrine, silvery with glass mosaic, shining bright like diamonds, or darkly like marcasite.

Night lent a softening, a blending, a new scintillation, and an added mystery. The hot, daytime mass of clearly seen intricacy was transformed to deeper majesty. The whole expressed a sublime imagery, every shape that sang out against the dark sky was mounting heavenwards, as Buddha himself in praise and symbolism.

We went down the dark stairs, again awed and stimulated. The ivory-carvers had long since gone home, and the flower sellers had packed up shop. So we returned to the ship to wash away the grime once more.

As we sailed the next day a new batch of deck passengers was settling in, a gypsy-like tribe of Nepalese, returning home after working at an up-country manganese mine. That night they slept in a crowded jumble, many unable to stretch out their legs, but their close-packed bodies made a decorative pattern, a kind of flowing fresco. The mass, snoring, unconscious movement, the delicious abandoned attitudes, the perpetual heaving, sighing and gentle swaying, the quiet co-operation of this giant family life was fascinating and touching to see.

We had sailed down the great, grey muddy Irrawaddy, and turned north for India, and it was at night—the first out at sea

again—that we heard with deep sorrow the radioed news of Lady
Louis' sudden death in Borneo. . . .

The gulls left us as we steamed up the Hoogli, and Brahminy
kites took their place circling overhead; unpleasant-looking birds
typical of the haunted life-in-death atmosphere of Calcutta.

I had stayed in Calcutta before, and although I had good
friends there my heart sank, I knew too well what it was like;
Stuart too had heard ominous stories of the difficulties of Calcutta
Customs, and of laborious bureaucracy likely to cause delay.

We wondered how long it would be before we could extricate
the Ark, repack and get on the road—the real road at last.

It took nearly all day to steam up the Hoogli. I had often seen
this vast Ganges Delta from the air, even in a Comet it seems to
take an astonishing time to fly across; today was a further con-
firmation of its colossal size.

With every passing hour the voices of the colourful gypsy-like
Nepalese on the after-hatch rose increasingly loud and shrill as the
ship drew closer to Calcutta. Pink and while balconied houses on
the river banks reminded me of Wathen's prints in his nineteenth
century journal of his voyage to India, Malacca and Macao. But
we were soon among sprawling slums, and at each lock, beggars,
jugglers and pathetically skinny boy tumblers assembled hopefully. Boys bathed in the foul dock waters; crowds of pedestrians
and cyclists waited at each opened bridge for the ship to pass.
Then suddenly there were men and girls running excitedly along
the roof-tops of ramshackle go-downs, waving and calling out to
friends on board. The *Sirdhana* had arrived; and this was the real
beginning of our venture.

❄ 3 ❄

From Calcutta to Astonishing Nepal

In Calcutta our Indian friends, the Dubes, and their friends too, did all they could to help entertain us, and to compensate for the delays. Basant and Savitri are Brahmins, fair-skinned and good-looking. She indeed is beautiful; she disliked Calcutta, and seemed not a little sad at having to live there. Basant is handsome and gay, and perhaps it is his high spirits that enable him to survive the grim city so well. His name means—spring; certainly in Calcutta it was the only touch of spring. Neither Stuart nor I could shake off the depression that Calcutta gives, and I know that we are far from being alone in this feeling; Indians and Europeans alike experience it.

For a week we went doggedly on : first striving to release Ark from the dockyard—redundant paper work, a mass of well-meaning officials, and a series of go-between agents made this a lengthy task. The simplest manoeuvre took literally hours, and hours grew into days.

Ark retrieved, our second task was to track down the Nepalese Consul in order to obtain visas for Nepal, unobtainable in Malaya. There was not a great deal of time left, there are only few planes a week from Patna to Nepal, and we hoped to catch the Wednesday flight.* To do so we should leave Calcutta at the very latest on the Monday. First there was a Nepalese holiday; then the Consul was away meeting an Ambassador; then it was Saturday and he had gone to the races. Finally, on the Sunday morning in despair we bribed a peon five rupees to take our passports to the Consul in bed. No doubt it was a highly unethical thing to do, but then, and only then, did Khatmandu come within our grasp.

Ark now stood ready packed in Basant's walled garden, every-

* We did not intend to drive to Nepal, partly because of the Ganges crossing at Patna, and partly because it was still rather early in the year for the mountain roads.

thing stowed away neatly, ready for the long trek at last, except that the promised locksmith had failed to arrive to repair a lock which had somehow been smashed on the roof-box.

To make sure we should never be without our 'chah', Basant made us a parting present of a great parcel of the best Darjeeling tea, and Savitri gave us three jars of her wonderful home-made chutney which enlivened many plain roadside meals later on. Basant's advice and suggestions proved invaluable, particularly the stress he laid on plans for a diversion to Madhya Pradesh. First to see the fabulous white tigers of Rewa, which had greatly impressed him; then to visit Savitri's parents, and finally to Orcha, a town over which he enthused. Basant had a favourite expression which had always tickled our fancy : — 'Lovely odour !' When he spoke rapturously of Orcha, his long full black eyes shining brighter than ever, 'Orcha !' he would exclaim, 'you simply mustn't miss Orcha—*lovely* odour !' But it is impossible to convey the aristocratic and sonorous roll of those expressive r's, and delicious aspirates, coming so enthusiastically from his handsome lips.

Monday morning dawned at last. The family watchman opened the gates, and we followed out in Basant's wake as he in his car guided Ark through the miles of drab lanes, and down to the Chowringhee with its wild taxis and ceaseless bleating horns.

But even then we could not leave. Another delay ensued over Income Tax forms which for some curious reason had to be filled in, and a final desperate search for a locksmith to repair that broken lock. We eventually ran one to earth, gathered him up and bore him with us plus all his tools to Ark standing conspicuous in the broad beflagged Chowringhee. I shall never forget that little Indian clinging like a gnome to Ark's roof-box, valiantly struggling to mend the broken lock while above him the flags were fluttering—Soviet and Indian—scarlet, green and gold, for that day Mr Kruschev was due to arrive.

We were becoming increasingly impatient; it seemed as if we should never get started. When finally the lock was mended it was late, so we decided to lunch first, and went to an hotel nearby.

We lunched quickly—praying no delay would crop up, for it seemed one never knew what could happen in Calcutta—and set off with a sigh of relief to drive out through the suburbs. It was said that when the Queen visited Calcutta the city's millions hid

their hovels simply by their packed ranks, but even when they are
not congregated, but moving about normally, one gets the impression of swarming humanity, living from hand to mouth. There
were refugees asleep on their packs; lean horses drawing aged
buggies. There were men trotting in perfect rhythm under the
weight of immense packing cases; men drinking tea out of tiny
earthenware cups; men in dhotis, boys in colourless garments,
beggars in rags; women in soiled white saris washing clothes at
broken standpipes in the pavements. And everywhere, of course,
cows and bulls, mostly grey white, the same drab as the saris and
the dhotis; and dogs from which it was best to avert one's eyes.
In these streets only the policemen were magnificent, they stood
out in their bright uniforms like a race apart, tall and well-fed.
Here and there a spot of comic relief on the hoardings lightened
the depression : 'Tabaksum Hair Oil—Good for the Hair and
Brain. . . .'

There was one brief and splendid view of Dakineswar, the great
Siva temple of The God in the South, across the Hoogli, and then
at last we drew away from the teeming city and were out in a more
open region; of bamboo and teak trees, and miles of harvested
paddy fields. The country folk in their poverty-stricken dress were
still as colourless but rather happier looking than the people of that
dreadful city. I had expected more colour; one thinks of India as
colourful, but after Malaya and Burma the drabness of Bengal
was overwhelming.

In the fields there were numerous deep-chested paddy egrets
which recalled Malacca's soft green acres and calm beauty, as also
the mango trees flowering now at the roadside in foam-like crowns
of pinkish and creamy white blossom. And for a while in this vast,
flat brown landscape I felt intensely homesick for the fresh green
beauty of Malaya, and her bright and colourful smiling people.
Dispirited as we both were by the week of frustration in Calcutta,
I was uncourageously inclined to look backwards, rather than
ahead—would all India be like this? I knew it could not be;
Basant himself had said that much of Bengal was beastly.* It was
he who persuaded us to go south off the Grand Trunk Road: there
we would see the true India.

* The best of Bengal lies in its cultural heritage. Had it been possible to
visit Tagore's Santinketan, or to make some literary contacts, no doubt I
should have seen even Calcutta in a rather different light.

At dusk the sight of Durgapur, the vast new steel project town, made us pause and stare. It stood a silver and flame inferno as startling as a thunderclap against a black western sky that, even as we looked, was cleft ominously with lightning. A sudden violent wind got up, flying sands and rain were blinding and it was, as Stuart said, only by a miracle of navigation that we eventually reached the bungalow of English friends, with whom we were to stay the night.

There was no time now to go to Bodh Gaya, and the next day was to be spent on the three hundred mile run to Patna. After a good sleep, and a good send-off our spirits began to rise. Gradually as the arid industrial country of East Bengal was left behind, the landscape became more attractive. Some of its scenes stand out vivid in my memory : a large herd of murrah buffalo winding along a dry river-bed jet black against parched sands; a small boy running on a high open space pursued by a tall dust-devil bearing a wild whorl of leaves in its vortex; the great Maithon dam project matching India's vastness, veiled in heat and dust. And nearer Patna—this was where we really began to enjoy life again—travellers reclining in palanquins borne by trotting barefoot men; tall slim riders on proud white horses with pricked ears, and scarlet trappings.

In the suburbs of Patna itself we crawled at pony pace through narrow streets among milling crowds, and nodding plumes and the jingles of pony bells. Ark passed slowly between tiny elevated shops open to the streets and on a level with our eyes, alive with flies and colour and glittering with enormous piles of glass bangles. Patna was preparing for the festival of Holi : yards of pale yellow and apricot-coloured saris were stretched like banners across the streets to dry in the sun; men's clothes were splashed with magenta inks, even some of the ponies' legs were pink-stained, indicating the advent of the spring festival from which we were to suffer later.

At Patna we heard there was bad weather over the mountains, planes were being turned back from Nepal.

In the morning there was a sudden last moment rush, for the airport telephoned earlier than was expected : the plane would after all be going. The hotel manager then said it was impossible for Ark to remain under the *cul-de-sac* porch; and this sudden parking problem nearly made us miss the airport bus. We were

People eating and
resting at the feet
of Buddha in a
Rangoon pagoda

A stall of flower
and paper offer-
ings in the Shwe
Dagon, Rangoon

Lunch-time
in Rangoon

This Gurkha
soldier's daughter
is a deck
passenger on the
way to India

slightly disconcerted at having to leave Ark in a nearby garage and hand over the keys to the hotel, and in the end we had to run. The bus was full of Russians also bound for Nepal, some of whom were most friendly, and interrupted our rather breathless discussion about Ark's safety with naïve admiration of our clothing, expressed in elaborate mime.

The weather over the mountains had not improved greatly, and now as the plane circled up over the Ganges, the sky ahead looming black as night, was stabbed with lightning. Over the high jungles of the Terai it looked for some moments as if the pilot was going to turn back, but soon we flew in over the vale towards Khatmandu. I stared down in surprise—for it was even more beautiful than I had imagined. Tiny houses stood compact and neat, like fourteenth century English cottages in mazy contours— the graded greens and browns of lovely terraced fields.

That afternoon Stuart and I were lucky to chance upon a most obliging trishaw wallah, Sira Baspur, a cheerful, robust Nepali boy. He had strong legs and lungs, and our only difficulty was to restrain him from cycling too fast. I will never forget that first ride, it was like plunging back into the Middle Ages as one entered the dark, narrow, crowded ways of the old town. The only touch of this day and age was the sound of our trishaw's horn, beeping furiously. Every alley and street was crowded with people moving in a brisk and constant stream. There were smiling faces, long dark eyes underlined with kohl, golden-faced children with bright red cheeks; giant Tibetans, striding along in their great felt boots; little Pahadi hill men and women, tramping in single file, bent nearly double under immense loads but chatting busily as they went.

Suddenly we burst into the first sunlit space, where the little golden shrine of Sitala, Goddess of Smallpox, shone with light. Black bulls and white cows wandered at will, rubbing past the shoppers, the files of laden hill people, the argumentative, playful Tibetans. I could feel my eyes widening; it was almost too much to absorb in one so rich and crowded a picture.

Here too was the Goddess of Famine's shrine, a three-tiered pagoda of red and gold smothered in fat smug pigeons—they at least would not starve. Famine held a silver bowl in her hands filled with food offerings on which the sparrows flocked to perch when the pigeons had dined. Beyond Famine were rows of money

c

changers, and here some young Tibetan refugees loitered, staring
too like us.

Every corner had a Siva shrine and its small kneeling Nandi
bull, the devoted stone vehicle of Siva. People were selling saffron
and chillies, and scarlet cords for plaiting in the hair—betel, hats,
cloth, brass. From under high dark gables women peeped out of
carved Newari windows, and all the time, flowing past, were men
carrying furniture, salt, carpets, quilts, ghee, curds, firewood, clay
pots from Badgaon.

Every now and again the enormous crescent-shaped horns of
the bulls showed upthrust among the white and black caps of the
Nepalese and the gold and scarlet fur-trimmed ones of the
Tibetans.

On the steps of a Siva shrine that was his den lay a blue-skinned,
near-naked Sadhu, sprawled on a leopard skin, aloof and patently
aware that his scornful individuality set him apart. Terrible, too,
for there was a hint, not of spirituality but of an archaic bestiality
in his expression and bearing.

It seemed to us both, later, that roughly assessing it there are
two aspects of Sadhuism : (we were to see more of this in Benares)
it seems that these rather terrible-looking Sadhus were possibly
members of the Aghori sect, among those who follow the left, or
black manifestations of Siva. We came, perhaps with over-simpli-
fication, to class the Sadhus merely as 'good' and 'bad'—the one
humble, quite modestly clothed; the other with a dreadful arro-
gance, a frightening glitter of self-exhibitionism in his ash-daubed
nakedness.

Then again we burst out of the narrow ways and were now in
the heart of Khatmandu, the Hanuman Dhoka, opposite the
great plaque of the 'black-faced terrible one'—Kala Bharaib
trampling the demons under his feet. Beyond this the cloaked and
reddened figure of Hanuman, the Monkey God, stood on guard
outside the old forbidden temple of the Kings. All around this
beautiful square were elegant five-tiered pagodas, gilded with gold
leaf, and painted dark wine-red.

We stopped our trishaw here, and got down to walk, avoiding
as we did so children defecating calmly here and there in this
Piccadilly of Nepal.

At one corner a tall building, with a deep-set portal caught our
interest : we wandered in through its doorway, and noticed a set

of immensely heavy wooden wheels lying in a room in the thickness of the walls. The inner courtyard was attractive and, rather
cautiously—for it is not long since Westerners were permitted
freedom in Khatmandu—we walked inside. We had a fleeting
glimpse of girls' faces, of reddened cheeks, a red dress in the small,
dark, lavishly carved window frames. A lean dog apparently dying
of ague lay on the stones of the courtyard. It was a beautiful dark,
decaying place, and we got the strong impression that it was a
brothel, but it was not—as we learnt shortly—it was the Kumari
Temple, home and virtual prison of the Living Goddess of
Khatmandu.

I think, from what I have since read, that on the first appearance at the window of the girl in red we should have bowed and
smiled—it was a pity that we didn't know in whose presence we
were when we walked into that courtyard.

The cult of the Living Goddess is, I think, peculiar to Nepal.
She is a ten-year-old girl chosen in babyhood for beauty, and
some say for courage in the face of masked devil dancers. She
reigns only for a short period : if she loses any serious amount of
blood, either from an accident or from natural causes, she ceases
to be Kumari, the virgin. So, at puberty she automatically resigns
her high office. Each little town in the vale has its own Kumari.
The antiquated, heavy wooden wheels which we saw in the gateway wall belonged to her gilded chariot, in which she is drawn
through the streets in procession by a team of men. In Pathan,
one of the little red and gold towns that flank Khatmandu, we
were lucky enough to see her carried on high—painted and
adorned, an exquisite little doll-like figure.

One afternoon we visited the ancient *chaitya* (a kind of vast
stupa) of Swayambunath, a well-known Buddhist place of pilgrimage, two thousand years old. It swarms with monkeys, is
ringed with prayer wheels, and adorned with Hindu as well as
Buddhist sacred statues and symbols—Sitala the Goddess of Smallpox has her shrine here, and Indra's golden thunderbolt provides
a play spot for cheeky monkeys. The prayer wheels are copper
cylinders stamped with Tibetan characters : — 'Om mani padme
hum', roughly 'Oh, God, the jewel (or soul), the lotus, so let it be
(amen)', often translated by Westerners as meaning 'the jewel in
the heart of the lotus', the spiritual element of God in man that
rises from the mire of the swamp. I like to think it means that,

though there is much argument about this famous little string of words. Anyhow, I rattled the prayer wheels hopefully, and must have said at least a million prayers by doing so—innumerable flags too fluttered over our heads, all of which represent prayers.

The Buddhism of Nepal is of the Mahayana or greater vehicle, and it has absorbed much of other faiths, such as the thunderbolt of Indra for example. And, being Tibetan-inspired, it is I believe lama-ised and threaded with animism, rather as Malayan Chinese Buddhism is interwoven with the 'magic' of debased Taoism, and of course influenced by Confucianism.

We called on the China Lama (whose family came from China many generations ago) at the *Chaitya* of Bodnath. This enormous white *chaitya* dates from the sixth or seventh century and is said to be the largest in existence. Although of a much later date than the Swayambunath it is in some ways more impressive, chiefly by its size and the purity of its enormous white dome so gaily be-flagged with prayer ribbons. The buildings encircling the great *chaitya* were then housing a vast number of Tibetan refugees, they crowded round pressing in, clamorous and good-natured, on all sides as we walked to the China Lama's house.

The China Lama, a smiling white-haired man, received us in his bedroom, which was draped in elaborate and garish brocades —the bed canopied, the floor carpeted in loud red rugs. As we spoke of Tibet and asked him about the refugees swarming outside under the gay prayer flags, he shook his venerable head, the light flashed on his little round golden cap, and he said sadly : — 'Now all the conditions of Tibet are finished—All is captured by Communism.'

Although he told us that he was 'speaking twenty-four lan-guages' we made little progress, and I suffered an acute sense of awkwardness—an uncomfortable suspicion that he might be somehow less holy than he made out. This was added to before we left by the hopeful attempt he made to sell us various expensive and undesirable souvenirs. But perhaps this was genuinely for the cause.

Several times we saw the great towering white peak of Himal Ganesh, but we never saw Everest and Annapurna, although we walked for miles into the hills one day beyond Navakot to a high col above the vale, where the view of these giants should have been perfect, but the clouds refused to lift and we had to return disappointed.

One of the most interesting places we visited in the vale was Pashupatinath, the most sacred of Hindu temples in Nepal; it was a good introduction to Benares.

We had already been to Pashupatinath but rather hurriedly, so on our last morning Stuart and I decided to return. Sira Baspur was summoned and we set off at a spanking pace. It was Sunday, a grey cold morning, but the sun began to shine as we arrived at the Monastery of the Fifth Paradise, where red pagodas guard the approach to the sacred Bagmati River and the shrines of Siva. The trishaw hurtled past the assembled beggars, and down a steep hill to the river. Rather resignedly we hoped that Sira Baspur kept his brakes in order, or else almost certain death awaited us at the bottom. This would have been appropriate had we been Hindus, for to die at Pashupatinath is to gain heaven indeed. To a good Hindu even to have visited Pashupatinath frees him from further incarnations in this world.

One small wooden pagoda near the beautiful stone bridge, has some typically erotic scenes carved and painted on its roof-supports. They depict rather orgiastic sexual unions, but it seems most likely that they are symbols of the union of the body and the spirit in the female aspect of Siva, that is the Shakti principle of female energy, which, combined with the male principles of destruction and of preservation are the source of all life in this world. Siva combines two conflicting forces—those of destruction, and those of preservation and recreation, here graphically symbolized, the orgies deriving probably from certain Tantric practices. The Chinese have for centuries expressed something of the same idea, only more delicately, in the Yang and the Yin symbol* which looks not unlike an eye, but which is evolved from the same principle of the balance of cosmic forces, the male and female elements, the light and the dark.

We walked onto the compact and lovely arch of a grey stone bridge and looked down into the Bagmati river. It runs out of the mountains here through a narrow gorge on its way across the vale, from which it delves through the southern hills to cascade to the jungles of the Terai and so eventually to reach the Holy Mother Ganges. Today only one body was burning on the ghats below the

* See the spine of this book.

bridge, its attendant male relative stood watching the flames and occasionally poking the corpse so that the smoke mounted up, drifting blue across the wine-red walls of the monastery and the little shrines with their erotic scenes.

The acrid stench of burning human flesh drove us away, and we turned to walk along the high unguarded terrace above the river. The terrace is wide, stone-flagged, and backed by rows of small Siva shrines each housing its lingam and yoni, the male and the female aspects of Siva, each pair watched over by their attendant adoring stone bull. Here previously we had been pestered by baksheesh boys, but today they were not bothersome, they seemed in an amiable mood, one child whistling away cheerfully and every now and again breaking into song. He had a clear, rather beguiling little voice that rang out over the river and reminded me of the Hindi songs I had heard so often in Malaya.

The main, very sacred shrine of Siva lay opposite the terrace across the river; the temple, approached by a long steep flight of steps, was crowned with a golden roof.

People came and went constantly. Some young Nepalese men ran gaily down the steep stairway, bearing trays of flowers which they splashed lightly with water from the holy river and turned to sprint back full tilt, as if they were racing each other to the temple above. A well-dressed family, the men in lounge suits, the women in bright coloured saris then appeared and rather cautiously dabbled their elegant fingers in the water, regardless of a thin ascetic who stood nearby stripping off his clothes. A monkey flung down a pot from a high balcony some fifty feet or more above the river. Another inquisitively followed a woman into a shrine as she went to bathe a lingam. On the roof tops a crowd of monkeys were eating and chattering. Then, sudden bedlam broke out, a protracted monkey battle ensued, and drifted down stream with squawks and shrill protests.

So all the time the life of this strangely lovely place—this deep wine-red, madder brown, gold and soft grey place—continued in its gay fashion, with the dead, the living, and the living-dead alike; its brown, swarming monkeys, its great statuesque jet black bulls, one of which, standing immobile on the curved stone bridge might have been Nandi himself waiting for the Lord Siva to appear in a clash of thunder. . . .

⚛ 4 ⚛

Holy Mother Ganges

While this journey was still in the planning stage a few pessimists had gone out of their way to prophesy various dire events which they expected would occur to ourselves and Ark: the main certainty being theft. When, on the morning we flew to Nepal, we had been obliged to leave Ark hurriedly and at the mercy of strangers, we did have some misgivings. But on our return to Patna, Ark had been driven back into the *cul-de-sac* at the hotel door, nothing inside her had been touched, and what was more, the watchman had given her a wash and polish.

I feel in the face of those gloomy warnings, it is worth recording that throughout the entire journey we lost nothing at all—except two small items through our own fault.

After drab Calcutta Nepal had refreshed us, we were now strong to face Benares; so the next day, though not without a certain amount of dread mingled with interest, we set off once more westwards on the Grand Trunk Road.

It was a greener countryside than the grim area near Durgapur, the roads were lined with trees of many kinds casting deep leafy patterns of shade across the hot surface. Winter wheat was ripening in the fields, and the sugar-cane harvest was in full swing: ox wagons loaded with canes were a minor hazard, Indian roads being mainly single track, so to pass a wagon one must horn furiously. In India it is not considered impolite to use the horn energetically, it seems to be expected; most of the buses and all the 'public' carriers have a notice on the rear—'Horn Please', and one takes advantage of the invitation. Bullock wagon drivers are often asleep, lying back flat out on their loaded carts, so it is advisable to start one's horning a long, long way behind them. If they happen to wake in time they may move off fairly smartly onto the earth side-tables, but one can never be certain to which side they will turn. If they do not wake up, there is nothing for it but to dash off onto the side-table oneself, and scrape past to a harsh rattling of those long, dry sugar-canes.

It had been raining in the night, and the side-table was deep in mud, mud that concealed an assortment of ironmongery, mostly nails cast off by oxen. Small wonder that we had our first puncture that day. It was an awkward one because, as the tyre subsided, Ark skidded half onto the side-table, where she had to remain as we changed the wheel. Lorries, buses and waggons were forced to circumnavigate us, but it was not long before a taxi driver stopped to lend a hand, and from then on we began to taste the true courtesy of the road.

Presently we were crawling at ox-waggon pace behind harvest carts over the three-quarter mile long bridge that spans the River Sone; road below, rail above. I was glad to go slow, for the vastness of the sandbanks, the serene lines of pool and stream lying against a level blue of distant trees beyond was beautiful under a gentle cloud perspective and the sky's wide arc above. In all these quiet level lines the only sign of life was a pounding of dhobis energetically torturing their laundry, some lazy white egrets, and a covey of vultures drying huge wings in the sun—each bird politely taking its turn to sit on and peck at the inflated belly of a dead cow stranded in one of the shallow streams of the Sone.

At Arrah there was again the jingle-jangle of pony harness, a sound now becoming familiar, and yet one that rang like a voice from earliest childhood. Again yards of coloured sari cloth hung across the streets to dry, and in the shops rope after rope of glass bangles added a touch of brittle gaiety.

We stopped at a garage to have the punctured tyre mended, and enquired the whereabouts of a historical monument known as 'The Little House at Arrah'. It happened to be in a nearby compound, part of some college grounds. A relic of the Mutiny, it is a small square building, held for one week in the hot season of 1857 by twelve Englishmen and fifty Sikhs against a body of two thousand sepoys and a large mob.

At a place called Hassanbazar a magnificent cattle fair was in progress. Hundreds of white cattle were herded together under the rich dark canopy of a grove of mango trees, where they stood a vibrant mass of light and shade, flecked with sunlight and blue shadow. Some were already being led away down the road; they were extremely nervous, as if they had never seen a car before, bucking at Ark although we slowed down to a crawl. Some of them had been blindfolded by their masters, many were decked with red cloth and strings of shells. This cattle mart appeared to be an entirely male affair, not a woman was in sight. Many white shirts and dhotis were splattered with the magenta pink, lemon yellow and peacock blue dyes of Holi. My handbook to India* calls Holi 'the Saturnalia of the vernal equinox, celebrated with the squirting or throwing of red and yellow powder. Servants should be warned to stay away'. Reading this, I recalled the amazement of Basant, and of other Indian friends that we should presume to travel without a servant. 'Where is your servant?' they would enquire, and on learning that we had none, they would ask in surprised, almost shocked voices: 'But *who* does the driving, the cooking, the washing . . . ?'

Nearing Benares later that afternoon we drove between fields of ripe corn; past a mud village, adobe gold in the westering sunlight, a mere huddle of warm brown roofs from which the temple *shikara* rose darkly against a flamboyant evening sky. The villages were few and far between now, the loneliness relieved by some giant monkeys gambolling and copulating under roadside trees. The sunset flamed gorgeously as perhaps only Indian sunsets can, and then, almost without warning we were on the bridge crossing the Ganges; and the whole sweeping curve of the laden riverfront, the steep ghats, the multitude of spires, unfolded below even as the huge ball of the sun was setting red behind the city.

It was an astonishing moment, and I knew at once that the beauty of Benares was going to outweigh, for me at least, its less pleasant aspects.

Stuart and I had long ago agreed to be extravagant in Benares, and had decided to stay at Clark's, one of the most famous hotels, I believe, in India. It lived up to its reputation, and we had a large and comfortable room where we could work in peace in intervals of almost unrelieved sightseeing.

We made arrangements to see the ghats with an official guide; for newcomers almost an essential in Benares, and we were lucky in our man, Abdul Hamid Khan, an ex-soldier who proved to be a real help, and who on no occasion detracted from the wonders by a spate of uncalled-for information.

Early the next morning the three of us squeezed into the front

* Murray's *Handbook to India, Pakistan, Burma and Ceylon.*

seat of Ark, and Stuart drove through the narrow ways of the old city, avoiding trams and buses, bulls and cows, and—as we drew nearer to the river—strings of pilgrims carrying flowers. Abdul Hamid did not always seem quite certain which was his left hand and which his right so that more than once Ark described a circle. However we eventually arrived near the Dasasvamedh Ghat, the Ghat of the Ten Horse Sacrifice, where sellers of flowers, of leaves, of peacocks' feathers wait to pounce upon the unwary, and where rows of pathetic and terrible beggars gather to line the approach to the river. This was the aspect that we had frankly dreaded, and here Abdul Hamil proved himself a great asset, effectively warding off the importuners, and with his aid we ran the gauntlet of the beggars.

There had been a rain storm in the night and the morning was cold and misty. How the pitiful half-naked beggars, the sick and the maimed, and the virtually naked 'blue' sadhus kept warm was a mystery. I suppose they simply did not. At any rate, for sadhus, especially those who are followers of Siva, self-mortification is part of life.

Curiously enough, informative books on contemporary India had been hard to find at that time, though I had searched in London and in Calcutta. So, before leaving Malaya I had written to Douglas Hill, a friend in England, to ask him for a few notes on Benares. A scholar of Urdu, Hindi, and Greek he had lived and worked for fourteen years as a schoolmaster in Benares, and he had responded with a long letter in the form of an essay. I shall quote from it here and there; for to my mind certain of his phrases have captured the feeling of that wonderful city far more succinctly than I could possibly hope to do after the ridiculously short time of three nights and two days, which was all that we could afford to spend there.

We walked down the ghats which were already milling with bathers despite the mistiness of the chilly morning. The river swirled past almost colourless, the bare eastern bank opposite lay half-hidden in ground mist. I shivered a little as we waited on the damp steps for a barge to come alongside.

The crowded curve of the western bank, with its splendid load of towers and temples, its encrustation of decaying palaces, steps and shrines directly faces that barren shore. Perhaps it is partly this dramatic contrast that makes the ghats so overwhelmingly impressive, at any hour of the day but most especially at sunrise. Douglas Hill wrote that the eastern bank is deserted because : 'Legend tells that it was cursed by Siva, who decreed that anyone dying on that bank would be born again as a donkey. Oddly enough the Maharaja's palace is on that bank, some distance from the river, but whenever he feels seedy he hastens to cross the river with his entourage lest he should wake to the world one day and bray. . . .'

It is claimed that Benares is the oldest city in the world, a claim made also for Damascus and Jericho and many other cities. But Benares is known to have been a living, vital centre since at least 600 B.C., and although it has of course changed, it has, unlike many other ancient cities, retained that vibrant humming life throughout the centuries.

The people of all India, of all sects and walks of life make Benares a place of pilgrimage; it is the most holy of all Hindu holy places. Many thousands of bathers come daily to the ghats starting from four o'clock in the morning, in a constant procession. It is this human aspect which makes the ghats one of the sights of this world, and which has endowed their worn grey stones with a remarkable aura, an atmosphere created through the ages by the extraordinary faith of all these myriads of people.

As the boatman rowed the small barge slowly up and down, the hum of Benares came loud and clear across the water. It was not as in most cities a hum of traffic, but of human voices; voices raised in prayer, voices laughing, calling, talking, begging, singing, chanting, and every now and again the silvery voice of a bell tolled out from some shrine or other; the bell that spoke most often was Sitala's, the Goddess of Smallpox. . . .

Further down stream beyond the main bathing ghats are the dhobi ghats, were rows of dhobis punish their vast piles of laundry on up-jutting stones. The entire steep ghat behind these busy men was covered with many-coloured saris spread out to dry. By now the sun had come through the mist and this array of colour made a vivid pattern. Insignificant in the shade of one corner the dhobis' weary-looking donkeys stood waiting to take home the great damp loads. Some young men were teasing a small and terrified donkey by tying a large tin can to its tail, and chasing it with stones down a slope. I wondered that it did not occur to them that the donkey might be the grandfather of one of them—had death taken place on the eastern bank.

Beyond the dhobi ghats and their suffering donkeys, the boatman turned the barge and rowed back slowly past the Ten Horse Ghat, towards the Mir Ghat. Now the bathers were more crowded even than before. They were of all classes and all shapes, rotund women, shapely girls revealing plump thighs and full dark-nippled breasts scarcely covered by thin saris; tall, slim brown young men exercising on the tops of stone buttresses dramatically silhouetted; fat elderly men; and lean, ascetic grey-haired men sitting in meditation on wooden piers above the river, their offerings of flowers drifting away below them. There were children too, naked, round, soft and dark, laughing and playing, or protesting loudly at being soaped and ritually bathed so cold and so early.

The Mir Ghat is I think the most beautiful, it has partly subsided into the river, and its broken stones and tilted shrines raise conical towers and sharp *shikaras* at picturesque angles from the water. Here we had the luck to witness the funeral of a 'good' sadhu. He belonged to one of the few classes of people whose bodies are not burnt on the ghats, but by custom consigned to Mother Ganges; saints, children under five, lepers, and those who have died of smallpox. Despite the bodies flung into the river, its sacred waters remain astoundingly pure and free from bad smells. And in any case, as my friend wrote, so absorbed are the countless bathers—'that during the influenza epidemic of 1918 when there was no time to finish off the bodies queueing up to be burnt, I have seen a bather impatiently pushing away a half-charred corpse with one hand while with the cupped right hand he drank the holy Ganges water. It is commonly said that the Ganges itself suffers no impurity but purifies all foulness that is thrown into its waters.'

When a sadhu is about to die he is made to sit up; no comfortable death for him; one leg must project straight out in front, the other is tucked into his groin; he must stiffen so, ready for his burial. The out-thrust leg will later be anchored to a stone, ensuring that his body shall sink to the bed of the river eighty feet down.

We watched his brethren in their apricot-coloured dhotis carry this body now, slung in its own matching robe along the ghats; the group made a delicate pageant of colour and movement against the pale ochreous stones. They carried him down to the river and began to prepare him for burial, scattering marigolds, washing him with holy water and all the time beating drums and blowing a conch shell, loudly and cheerfully. A great stone was fixed to the stiffened leg and then the body, now tied in its apricot shroud, was taken out in a rowing boat and flung into the Ganges with a resounding splash. A few marigolds rapidly drifting downsteam on the current were all that briefly marked his grave.

A little further upstream, at the Jalsain Ghat, the Burning Ghat, some forty or fifty bodies are cremated daily. We saw three small boys standing beside somebody's pyre, casually drying their pants and g-strings after a swim while the shaven-headed nearest relative poked the burning logs, and a dog routed hopefully in neighbouring ashes. Here too a cow stood placidly chewing the cud beside the unlit pyre of a woman with garlanded feet, another corpse awaiting its fire — a woman's body is shrouded in red, a man's in white.

Behind a small breakwater where the last remains are flung one of the firemen squatted, methodically sifting ashes.

When I asked what he was doing, Abdul Hamid ordered the boatman to row closer. The fireman looked up into our faces with a wide, knowing grin; his small black eyes glittered as he held up a gold ear-stud between his dark fingers. We were told that it is his right to sift the ashes after each cremation, to find and to keep any gold ear-studs or nose rings, small earthly possessions of the deceased. Although by Mr Nehru's decree it is no longer permissible to speak of caste in India, these firemen and pyre builders come from what was once considered a very low caste indeed — the Doms (from whom the Romanys are probably descended; the hard D of Hindi being more closely akin to our R than our D). It is, says Douglas Hill, their monopoly to supply the fire for the corpses and they certainly grow fat on this. 'They are addressed as *Maharaj* — I always imagine that this is not a term of respect but of irony mixed with some superstitious fear.' Our guide told us that as they have this monopoly in the fire business they can and sometimes do demand large sums; it is said that they have great wealth and possessions and that several of the decaying palaces here belong to them.

When the fire is received from the fireman, the eldest son applies the torch and as Douglas Hill wrote: 'he then breaks the skull with a long pole. This is said to release the spirit, but it is, in fact, necessary, lest the head should burst like a hot chestnut and scatter the brains. . . . I was once escorting the wife of the Bishop of Bombay on a boat in the early morning. Thinking that a crema- tion on the Burning Ghat was a rather unpleasant sight for Her Holiness, I tried to draw her attention away to a palace nearby. Receiving no reply, I found her eyes fixed on the performance at the pyre, as she murmured, "I see they don't mind *poking* poor Willie . . .!" '

Bodies burn daylong on this ghat, the relatives must poke them to accelerate the process, and I saw them making a neat pile of rib-cage, pelvis and skull as one would deal with autumn leaves and rubbish on a bonfire in an English garden. No doubt that is their feeling, wisely enough—the body is nothing but an autumn leaf. It is, after all, the soul that matters, it will go on into another life, or here by the holy river it has perhaps at last attained Nirvana.

Above the door of the 'Golden Temple' is a figure of Ganesh bathed in Ganges water by the pilgrims. For some reason our guide called him 'Saturday's God who takes away trouble'; he is the remover of obstacles, the god of travellers, the elephant-headed son of Siva. Near the door was a large notice which said : 'Gentle- men not belonging to the Hindu religion are not allowed inside.' But we were able to squeeze through a narrow passage to the right of the temple, which although paved was swimming in mud and Ganges water. Halfway down we were allowed to peep through a small grid, but I could see only a seething mass of bare feet, and the hems of dhotis and saris. The noise was deafening, and as near to babel I think as anything I have yet heard. A constant stream of pilgrims yelled and crashed their way through this holiest of holies; for a special festival, I thought, but we were told that every day it was the same.

We emerged thankfully from that booming alley-way, but the ear-splitting racket scarcely lessened. We were now in a quad- rangle called the Gyan Kup—the Well of Knowledge. It was crowded with pilgrims who strolled, walked, or charged round the Well of Knowledge, and we were swept up with them, past a huge red seven-foot Siva bull. There were more beggars, garlanded men, sadhus, women and children, cows and bulls, trays of flowers and of sweetmeats; and all the little white feet of the gods were covered in petals. In the hot sunlight and also in the flickering shade of a peepul tree, rows of blood red and dusky orange powders heaped upon trays struck out as notes of pure unadulterated colour.

Of the tree Douglas Hill says: 'The chief property of this particular peepul, or sacred fig tree, is the destruction of anyone who tells a lie when beneath its shade,' adding with a customary touch of cynicism — 'Apparently it doesn't matter if one tells a lie anywhere else. . . .'

Sights, sounds and scents were all so loud and so strong that one felt the senses violently assaulted, and craved for respite, a quiet place from which to gaze and to absorb more slowly some of this agitating brilliance. The place was right at hand: beyond the peepul tree was the Mosque of Alamgir; our guide led the way to a side gate, gratefully we mounted the steps and took off our sandals. The courtyard was hot and clean and dry in the sunlight, and above all it was quiet. I have never seen the contrast between the Hindu and the Muslim religions more clearly marked. The imam came forward and received us smilingly, and we went inside the peaceful cool interior for a few moments.

But the stunning contrast of those two holy places was perhaps even more evident when we retraced our steps. On the far side of the lane opposite the main gate of the 'Golden Temple', there was a shrine of sorts, a kind of club for musicians, the 'good' sadhu in charge of it appeared to be a friend of Abdul Hamid, and we were allowed upstairs to a small balcony. From here, the view of the crowded alley-way below was fascinating, and that of the splendid domes and golden *shikaras* of the temple now only a few feet from where we stood. Behind their sun-drenched gold, the pure white minarets of the Alamgir Mosque soared against the glowing blue of an Indian midday sky; the glittering domes in juxtaposition with the soaring purity.

Tired, enriched, excited, we returned to the hotel, through teeming streets; Abdul Hamid saying right when he meant left, Stuart alert and patient at the wheel. Clark's Hotel, with its flowers, long cool verandahs, and decorative Indian servants was a far cry from the ghats, the city, and the corpses — it was another world. When we had washed and changed we sat in the bar to recover over iced gin, both feeling a little stunned by all we had seen. It needed some digesting.

Then we saw across the room the familiar bearded face of a

man we knew—Dr Molesworth once of the Sungei Buloh Leper
Settlement near Kuala Lumpur, and he came to join us for a
drink. I wanted to know about some of the beggars, whom I presumed were lepers at the ghats, and he was just the man to ask.
He assured me that few of them were in fact lepers; he said that
a great many of these people were self-mutilated, and—what was
worse—some had been deliberately mutilated in childhood by
their own parents so that they might become professional beggars.
This almost unbelievable horror I found hard to accept but I fear
that it is true.

One afternoon we went to Sarnath, the Buddhist shrine once a
deer park, where Buddha preached his first sermon. It was a quiet,
peaceful place; Asoka's beautiful lion pillar was magnificent, and
Stuart was fascinated by the ancient brick stupa, compact and
solid in a neat rose garden among the excavations—all in sharp
contrast with the hubbub of the ghats. There was a Jain temple
there, and also a modern Buddhist one, the walls of which were
painted with huge morals by a Japanese artist, Kosetu Noso.

There were several Tibetans in the gardens with some charming
friendly children, and inside the modern temple a Tibetan couple
were praying devoutly—a long-haired young man and a girl. As
I walked round softly on bare feet looking at the murals, I heard
a reiterated oddly jangling little sound, and it was a second or two
before I realized that it was caused by the Tibetan girl—each
time she bowed herself in prayer her long silver ear-rings thumped
heavily on the marble floor.

Later that afternoon we returned to the ghats, this time to walk
a mile or so along them at sunset when the golden light falls cross-
ways on the steps and terraces. It was the hour during which the
widows congregate around their guru, to chant and sing.
Numerous preachers under giant straw umbrellas read from the
scriptures, and give advice in loud sonorous voices to their followers, while Sitala's bell rings out constantly. Through the shrine
of Mother Ganges, who rides on a crocodile's back, a half-naked
young man strode like a god. On the steps, an antelope, the so-
called 'sacred wild cow', the nilgai, wandered at will, and came
to nuzzle at our hands.

We walked above the burning ghats, where a huge notice for-
bids photography, but as it says nothing about drawing, I man-

Vegetables for sale
in a Nepalese
market

Shopping by night
in old Khatmandu

A spring scene
near
Khatmandu

A sari weaver in
Benaras

aged to do a quick sketch. The man that I drew looked uncomfortably alive on his pyre, as if he were trying to thrust away the burning logs from off his chest.

It was nearly dark by the time we reached the Manikarnika, most sacred of all the ghats; *mani* means jewel, *karni* an ear : Parvati, wife of Mahadeo is said to have dropped her ear-ring here, and Mahadeo in searching for it dug a great hole in the ground—the origin of the deep tank on the terrace. In the rapidly gathering dusk we went to look down into the Well of the Jewel, and saw the smiling faces of young men and girls gazing up from far below. They were decorating the well with marigolds and jasmine; they had covered the steps with pink cotton, stretched an awning above, and set a wooden structure like a pergola in the bottom for flowers in readiness for the festival of Holi.

As we stood looking down, a man descended into the tank carrying a lantern, its warm rays cast long fingers of light and shadow on the figures and the flowers below.

Then we turned away again, into the heart of the city, and would instantly have been lost but for Abdul Hamid, who guided us rapidly through narrow, black alley-ways where temples and dwellings, storehouses and shrines loomed dark and mysterious like cliffs above our heads. Soon we reached the 'Golden Temple' still loud with voices; and the little shops, bright now with lamps, and the colour of baubles, fruit and flowers.

On the last morning we got up at five o'clock to see the sunrise over the eastern bank. It was a perfect morning; already countless people were bathing and, as the sun began to rise, they lifted their hands repeatedly in prayer, cupping the water of the river in their palms. The widows with their shining brass pots were grouped together waiting for the day; as Sitala's first bell rang out a great flight of pigeons wheeled away over the ghats welcoming the dawn, and hundreds upon hundreds of people stood facing east as the huge ball of the sun rose clear of the deserted eastern shore, to touch the city and the bathers with gold. Then at once the hum of a new day's voice grew louder and more insistent from the crowded western bank.

D

⚛ 5 ⚛

Off the Grand Trunk Road

From Benares we made our second diversion off the Grand Trunk Road, south west, into Madhya Pradesh to see the Rewa Maharaja's fabulous white tigers—and the deeper we travelled into India so her fascination grew.

We had scarcely arrived in Rewa when we met the first link in the marvellous chain of welcome that we were to receive everywhere in hospitable Madhya Pradesh. Basant had written of our plans to his father-in-law, Mr Pathak, State Collector of Tikamgarh many miles away to the south. It was Mr Pathak who made it possible for us to stay in the Circuit House (Circuit Houses are normally reserved for judges and Government officers on tour), and he had written to a colleague and friend in Rewa, who had sent an invitation to dine that evening, and also arranged for a young man to act as guide to the Maharaja's palace the following morning.

Mr Pathak's friend lived in a little square-topped house, to which his bearer led us when we had bathed and changed, where his wife provided a most delicious dinner. I had already noticed that although Indian ladies never *have* to serve their own meals, as so many of their counterparts must nowadays in England, they do most often taken an active part in preparing the food.

In my opinion, for variety, subtlety and excellence, at its best Indian cooking ranks next only to Chinese. We found after leaving India the standard rapidly deteriorated, and not until we encountered French cooking once or twice in the Lebanon, was there anything even approaching its quality again until we reached France, at the end of the 12,500-mile journey.

The morning dawned cold, for Rewa lies at over a thousand feet above sea-level. The Circuit House, a relic of the British era, stood in the grounds of the former residency. We walked along its pleasant avenues of mango trees, mourning a little for the passing of that era, with a peculiar almost apologetic sense, born half of

patriotism and half of inherited guilt which forcibly assailed us
both many times in India, and later in Pakistan too. It was a
curiously mixed sensation. For we had never experienced any of
this guilt sense in Malaya; but it is well known that the short
British régime there was, and always had been—except for the
bad post-war blunder of 'Macmichaelism'—on a vastly different
footing from that of the Raj in India.

The young man who was to guide us arrived at seven a.m., and
we left in Ark for the palace. It was important to be there before
seven-thirty, because for an obscure reason, the tigers had a rooted
objection to visitors after eight o'clock. They also disliked black,
as I soon found out to my discomfort; I happened to be wearing a
black sweater and had to shed it before we were allowed anywhere
near the den, because they had once leapt at a Minister of State
carrying a black umbrella. So, shivering, I prepared for the approach. It took some time : first an aged man went away to fetch
a bunch of enormous keys, then we followed him as one by one he
undid the gigantic Indian padlocks, and opened a series of doors,
until at last we were in a dark passage-way giving onto a garden
of bamboos and shrubs. The tiger smell was strong and acrid. The
old man's last key grated in another lock, an iron door swung
open, and he slipped inside, beckoning us to follow.

The room was almost pitch-dark, but as my eyes grew used to
it, I noticed a grille in the wall opposite; following the old man's
directions I went close to this . Immediately a great white face
came snarling up against the bars. Naturally, I recoiled pretty
quickly, but then as the tiger padded softly away, I stared through
again. He was a superb creature; big, sleek, blue-white in his
shadowy den.

He had been caught in the local jungles by the Maharaja about
ten years previously when just full-grown. His mate was an
ordinary tigress, a fine one, but beside his chimerical beauty, his
delicate otherworldly colouring, her warm golden coat looked
merely commonplace.

The pair had already had several litters, all golden until just
over a year previously, when the tigress gave birth to four perfect
white cubs.

The cubs lived in a large separate den across the garden; more
obliging than their parents they presently came out to play; yawn-
ing, stretching and snarling a little, while waiting for breakfast.

They were in excellent condition. Striped black in the usual manner and, apart from their strange colouring, there was nothing abnormal about them. They were big, considerably more than half-grown, and entrancingly beautiful. Three had green eyes, but the fourth had a pair as blue as any well-bred Siamese cat. They were certainly not albinos. Basant had been quite right, they were well worth the diversion. But to our disappointment we were not allowed to take photographs.

In the sunlight, their strange coats made them look like enormous Siamese cats. In the shade they turned to a bluish white, as if they were moon creatures from some antique forest of fantasy. In their own jungle setting, they would indeed have the appearance of the supernatural, especially on a moonlight night.

The Maharaja did not live in the royal palace of his ancestors, but in a small modern house across the moat. The tigers seemed to have the old palace more or less to themselves except for their keepers, and an ancient caretaker. The moat was five miles in circumference, and four hundred yards wide. On one side of it were citrus orchards and spring blossom, on the far side, fields of ripening winter wheat led to the low ranges of forested hills beyond, the natural hunting-ground of tigers.

A large boathouse sheltered an interesting little fleet of pleasure boats, one was particularly attractive, in fact quite a museum piece. It was a hundred-year-old paddleboat with a canopied throne, and a small balconied space for musicians and singers. It was man-powered; the paddles worked by six men treading in barefoot rhythm on silent, smooth-running blades behind the throne, so that no offensive mechanical noises would detract from the gentle lap of water, or from the voices of musicians singing before the throne.

After we had seen over the palace and the boathouse, we were taken to breakfast with some young agricultural officers in a cottage garden surrounded by orchards. I think it was the young men's 'elevenses', for breakfast is not really an oriental meal. The only trouble was the flies, but we did our best not to notice them and ate what we could of the hard-boiled eggs, curried millet, vegetarian curry puffs, nuts and ghee and sweetmeats and papaya —all of which had been set out so carefully among the flowers. The young agriculturists were most friendly; pressing us to accept the addresses of friends and relations in places ahead.

After breakfast we set off for the temples of Khajuraoh. It was a perfect Indian spring day, the sky a cloudless blue. We met little or no traffic here off the Grand Trunk Road, and we felt happy and in high spirits. The thread was loosening, and at last I was not looking back in regret at the life we had relinquished, irrevocably.

There were avenues of flowering trees, and in the wilder open places more and more of the apricot-red flamboyant flowers blooming on stark grey bare branches. The blue wings of Krishna's lovely birds flashed often across the way, and once a deer startled by our engine bounded off wildly over the fields of winter wheat. At last this was the open countryside, the real India, we supposed, and yet to us both it was somehow not quite oriental, being so unlike the East as we had known it for years; there was even a hint of Europe in those wide fields of wheat. Again I wondered, where, in fact, *does* the real East begin? And where the Far East . . .?

Khajuraoh was once the ancient capital of the province of Jejahuti, first mentioned by that remarkable seventh century Chinese traveller, Hiuen Tsang, whose name crops up in many fascinating places in the Orient; in Khatmandu, and as far away as Angkor in Cambodia. But he could not have seen the temples of Khajuraoh as they are today, for they were mostly built between A.D. 950 and 1050 by rulers of the Chandel dynasty.

The modern village of Khajuraoh is tiny. We arrived there late that golden afternoon; it was the Friday before the Holi moon, and everyone was in holiday mood. To the left of the road the *shikaras* of numerous temples glowed darkly against the westering light. Their roofs rose layer upon layer, like the foothills of the Himalayas—which they are intended to represent—mounting to a final peak rising into the serene blue sky, symbolizing man's eternal aspirations. And on their walls are thousands of carvings. They did in some respects remind me a little of Angkor, but unlike Angkor, where the temples face west as monuments of death, nearly all these face east; one is dedicated to Surya, the sun god.

At the small Resthouse there was a little crowd of friendly Indians, sitting with their families, drinking tea under the graceful down-drooping branches of a grove of *mahua* trees in the golden light; and—not a tourist to be seen.

Again Mr Pathak's welcome reached out. He had sent a bearer, and an enormous basket containing one dozen quart bottles of beer. We were unable to converse much with the bearer, but he was an amiable country boy with a friendly smile; he was often a help, and during the wildness of Holi when Ark was smothered in cow dung by small boys, his services proved extremely useful. We appreciated the lavish 'do unto others' hospitality of the real India.

The weather remained glorious, the perfection of those Indian spring nights with the Holi moon rising to the full and the fresh, sparkling mornings held a never-to-be-forgotten ambience. That weekend stands out in memory for us both as one of the highlights of our journey. We spent nearly the whole time, two and a half days, in the northern group of temples; the serene atmosphere was conducive to work; the garden was entirely free from beggars and guides, and for the greater part of the time we had the temples almost to ourselves. Their structure is cruciform; a series of mandapas lead in from the steps to the cella, under the mounting crests of the roof. Their sandstone is a soft buff colour, warm and mellow, glowing and changing with the moods of the Indian sun. Each stands on a lofty terrace, above which the mass of the build-ing rises; compact, elegant and wonderfully proportioned, in a series of mouldings, to the walls and balconied openings of the interior. Two, or often three bands of magnificent carvings then lead the eye upwards to the mounting rooftop culminating in its final graceful *shikara*.

On the Kandariya Mahadeo temple alone it is said that there are 872 figures. In my opinion, this was the most lovely of all and as it was in the process of being cleaned, an elaborate though rickety scaffolding against its side enabled me to climb close to the bands of carving to make studies of these erotic but elegant heavenly beings.

On the Saturday a few Indian soldiers wandered round the temples, and presently two of their officers invited us to drinks with them in their camp that evening. They were of the Kumaon Regiment, on their way home after extensive exercises deep in the great central state.

Their camp was only just down the road but so well camou-flaged that we overshot it at dusk, and nearly did not arrive, for Ark suddenly developed a crippling electrical fault. We were just able to crawl back along the road and, as the full moon rose above the trees, we spotted the camp. While we sat talking and drinking in a circle in front of shadowy tents and trucks, engineers did their best to repair Ark's fault; the officers were concerned because their electrician was away ill.

Despite its camp formality that little cocktail party was conducted with traditional Sandhurst-trained bearing and etiquette, the officers seemed more British than the British themselves and were remarkably good to look at with their long, dark eyes and aristocratic Moghul features. It was a splendid setting; the rim of black trees, a clear sky and the great moon of Holi. Saturday night in Khajuraoh—what more could one ask for at that moment? I leant back in my chair, at peace with myself and the world, exhilarated by the rare beauty, my body pleasantly tired, lulled in the moonlight, and still glowing from the long day in the spring sunshine.

After a last morning spent among the gods and long-eyed heavenly lovers we reluctantly turned our backs on Khajuraoh, and set off again to the west, for Tikamgarh, Mr Pathak's home. Khajuraoh was farewell to the best of the Hindu element, architecturally speaking and nothing was to move me again so deeply until we reached Isfahan.

Mr Pathak's neat white house stood in the same compound as the Circuit house where we slept in a vast Victorian suite, though we took most of our meals with him. He was a very tall, handsome man, with a shy wife, and another pretty daughter—sister to Savitri.

Mr Pathak had two good friends; one tall and slim, the other short and stocky, the latter, Mr Hiremath, had a most lively sense of humour. He was one of those endearing personalities who have that extraordinary power of making people laugh, merely it would seem, by their presence. These friends called themselves 'the Three Musketeers'.

When we had bathed we went across the courtyard to Mr Pathak's house, where we sat in the garden until the night grew too chilly; as we talked the great moon rose, coppery gold above the mango trees and shone on Mr Pathak's own little field of ripe wheat and ripening dahl at the end of the garden. We were plied with generous pegs of whisky, and made to feel that this was a festive occasion : I remember there was much laughter, especially at the remarks of the bubblingly amusing Mr Hiremath, a Yogi exponent.

Shy Mrs Pathak would not sit down to dinner with us, but she produced a succession of dishes so out of this world that even the memory of them now makes my mouth water. The blue-washed dining-room was simple and pleasing. In one corner, in an old punkah rope hole in the wall, a tame sparrow nested, he popped out several times during the course of that lengthy meal, and was obviously much at home. Afterwards we washed our hands under a brass pot, allowing the water to fall into a bowl of leaves and flowers set specially for this purpose; and eventually retired, rather merrily, across the moon-flooded courtyard to the Circuit House and our vast Victorian suite.

Mr Pathak devoted the whole of the next day to showing us something of his district. We went first to an experimental Government citrus orchard, where there was a mouldering little cottage, constructed of 36,000 empty whisky bottles. With the faint hangover from which I was suffering, the sight was not very welcome. I forget who had built the place but, I should think, he died of D.T.'s long ago, and is probably now working out his *karma* as a drawer of water, poor fellow.

A man ran forward to set a table and chairs in the deep shade of a great mango tree, and another brought a tray of fruit decorated with marigolds, jasmine and roses. We walked a little way among the citrus trees, and plucked some small sweet lemons, which were delicious; they reminded me of the tiny *sambal* oranges that are eaten with Malay curries in Malacca. We went away laden with lemons, grapefruit, oranges, and flowers heaped on leaves. Everywhere we went that day, I was given flowers in tiny posies, or piled on boat-shaped leaves.

Tikamargh is named after an appellation of Krishna (Ranchor Tikam), and *garh,* a fort. Those delightful birds, known as Krishna birds (I was never able to discover their true name) were numerous here. Slightly larger than thrushes, their lovely cerulean blue plumage contrasted well with the golden fields. Mr Pathak said that it was considered lucky to see them early in the morning. Their colour was a joy itself, and we came to look for them gladly at the start of each new day on the road. We continued to meet them on and off, or at least their slimmer cousins as far as eastern Greece; like the decorative hoopoe, another very lovely bird, they are widespread. Krishna, the fluting cowherd god is one of the most pleasing of Hindu deities, much loved by country folk and of course by women : — 'lover of 16,000 milkmaids'.

This was dacoit country, and it was partly for that reason that Basant had advised us not to camp by the roadside. Perhaps he was right, and indeed Mr Pathak said that there were still four or five active major gangs of dacoits, whom it was difficult to subdue, as they work upon a kind of Robin Hood system which naturally appeals to the poverty-stricken peasant.

That we were never brave enough to camp anywhere in India or Pakistan is now one of our regrets. I am certain had we travelled in the reverse direction, we should have become so used to camping in various conditions that we should probably have done so, if not in dacoit country, elsewhere in India. But at the start of the journey we were reluctant to go against the advice of men such as Basant : therefore in India not only did we spend money on hotels out of all proportion to the rest of the journey, but we also lost that sense of oneness with a land that can only be achieved by long evenings, nights and dawns spent out in the open country-side.

In the yard of one rambling great fort we visited that morning, we almost stumbled over a whole nest of little seventeenth century cannon balls. Mr Pathak made us a present of one for our sons, the first of an odd collection of weighty objects with which the accommodating Ark gradually became burdened.

At lunch time Mrs Pathak provided another wonderful meal, and in the afternoon and early evening there was a royal shooting lodge to see, palaces besides vast tanks, mongoose on the roads, herons, cranes, and—at an ancient and enchanting riverside temple—wild peacocks strutting in deep tree shade.

The following day we left Tikamgarh for Orcha of 'lovely odour' fame; Mr Pathak and Mr Hiremath accompanying us in Ark, having sent their cars on ahead, and we drove on a new jungle track.

Our first sight of Orcha was across the wide Betwa River. The fort, seventeenth century palace and a row of temples reared, dark and lovely shapes, into the hot, blue sky. As we got out to stand and admire, a crowd of men and women pilgrims, dressed in white, and in wine-red came up from the river where they had been bathing and resting. When they had satisfied their curiosity

for a few moments, they obeyed Mr Pathak, and obligingly moved
off across the magnificent stone causeway, giving life and colour
to that splendid setting, the vast river and towering buildings on
the high bank beyond. The causeway is known as the Golden
Bridge, and the Kanchan Ghat beyond it, the Golden Bathing
Ghat, was so called, said Mr Pathak surprisingly, 'because of the
gold dust washed off all the ladies bathing there.'

The Chaturbhuj temple, object of the pilgrimages, is the only
one in all India, Mr Pathak told us, where Rama is worshipped
in the form of the raja. Idols of the raja and his consort stand in
place of the usual gods and goddesses. As we were with Mr Pathak
we were allowed into the inner shrine itself to pay homage to the
small, bedecked doll-like figures. I clasped my hands together in
the *namaskar,* Indian fashion and retreated backwards as best I
could.

After a hilarious farewell lunch at a remarkably Victorian hotel
in Jhansi Mr Hiremath, nothing daunted by the amount of beer
he had drunk, stood on his head and in this position proceeded to
demonstrate Yoga movements under the glassy-eyed stare of tiger,
deer, wild cattle and other stuffed trophies glaring disdainfully
from the walls.

That evening at Gwalior we met three Australians who had just
come through Persia and Pakistan, and had found the high passes
still deep in snow. Though they'd had no serious mishaps I
gathered it had not been at all pleasant, and they said, with a
meaning look at me, that this was much too tough a journey for
women; *they* had sent their wives on by sea.

Next morning, two very talkative young men arrived—professors, they said, one of history and one of psychology, and they had
been asked, I think by Mr Pathak, to escort us on a sightseeing
tour.

Gwalior is famous mainly for its fortress, on an impressive
'precipitous, flat-topped isolated hill of sandstone', three hundred
feet above the town; and for its colossal rock sculptures.

We went first to the top of the plateau to look at the Chit
Mandir, or Painted Palace, in which was a horrible circular
dungeon, above a firehole where women were expected to commit
sati when defeat of their own forces appeared imminent.

There were some lovely little eleventh century Hindu temples,
the Sasbahu, mother and daughter-in-law temples standing side

by side : one was in the cruciform style of Khajuraoh but not as beautiful.

The sightseeing over, our two young professors who seemed to know little of either history or psychology, insisted that Stuart should drive into the heart of Gwalior to buy some concoction of curds, milk and mangoes which was apparently peculiar to the town. I am sure they meant well, but they would take no refusal, though neither of us could face the thought of milk and said so — the one thing we are really squeamish about in the East. Squalid Gwalior : the slums and bazaars were alive with uninhibited Holi boys and men; it was no place to take an obviously foreign car, always easy prey at the height of that saturnalia. The professors must surely have been aware of this; but perhaps they wanted us to savour the full impact of Holi, or perhaps they really wanted their curds and mango juice. Just in time, we closed the windows as the coloured fluids came streaming fast; scarlet, peacock-blue, lemon-yellow and purple, all over the van, repeatedly flooding across the windscreen — making one see red quite literally.

I know one is supposed to take Holi in good part, but at one point I found it hard to keep my temper; as Stuart, blinded by prolonged and violent washes of colour, gritted his teeth, swore loudly and slowed to a snail's pace to avoid killing the revellers.

We left 'Gwalior-Squalior', as Stuart dubbed it, most gladly as soon as possible after a hurried lunch. On the road again, Ark looking like something out of a fairground roused many a laughing jibe.

When we arrived at Laurie's Hotel, in Agra, a Muslim car-cleaner immediately offered his services as we drew up outside a bungalow suite in a flowery garden. He took one look at our highly-coloured vehicle and said : —

'Car play Holi?'

✳ 6 ✳

Agra and Delhi

The car-cleaner's question had been entirely rhetorical of course, but there was genuine sympathy in his voice and perhaps some personal feeling too, for it was to take him the best part of two days to remove all traces of the coloured deluge.

After the succession of clear and glorious sunsets in Madhya Pradesh, that first evening the Shah Jahan Gardens was disappointingly grey. But the Taj stood gorgeous in its huge simplicity, the great dome almost silvery white against a pearly sky, its quiet reflections unruffled in the pools below, framed in dark lines of cypresses where once Shah Jahan had grown his peach trees.

Behind the wide marble terrace of the Taj the Jumna flows through sandbanks and cultivated lands in a wide and lovely curve. From the terrace we looked across the river to the flat land opposite on which Shah Jahan had planned to build his own mausoleum — a black one, as supreme complement or 'answer' to the white purity of the Taj. *'Jawab'* was the word he used, an Arabic one familiar to me through Malay in which it also means answer; and akin too surely to the *shawabtis*, or 'answerers' of ancient Egyptian tombs. The great spread of Arabic influence under Islam's vast span was once again brought home to me.

But Shah Jahan did not live long enough to carry out his plan of building a black *'jawab'*. It would perhaps have been almost too perfect, a dare to the divine, a vast Yin and Yang face to face across the Jumna but divided in death. Perhaps he preferred to be buried, as in the end he was, next to his Mumtaz Mahal — his 'elect of the palace'. His favourite queen — she married him in 1615 and significantly she died in childbirth of her fourteenth child, just fourteen years later.

His face is that of an eager passionate dreamer, an ardent poet, as befits a man who killed by his desire the object of his love, and who created to her memory the poem in marble that is the Taj.

Its beauty grows upon one each time one sees it, in much the same way as the beauty of the Parthenon does; although, of course, no two buildings could possibly be more different.

The following morning we went to the Gardens before day-break to watch the rising sun touch to gold eastern facing walls, facets and minarets, while the birds awoke in the trees. Flocks of green parakeets began then to swoop about the garden paths with the doves and the crows, and some little bouncy birds, the name of which we did not know. Stuart dubbed them 'pogo-stick birds', because of their peculiar gait.

Agra's birds were delightful: in the hotel garden near our verandah a large tray had been fixed on a pedestal, and each morning immediately it was filled with food a gay mob of green parakeets flew down to crowd there.

Having missed the full moon by our Madhya Pradesh detour we realized that we should not be able to see the Taj by moon-light, as every visitor should—unless we got up at half-past one in the morning as a last resort. So we duly roused ourselves at this horrible hour, dragged on layers of clothes over our pyjamas for the night was cold, and set out determinedly, driving through deserted roads.

The waning moon was shining brightly and we began to congratulate each other, sleepy though we were. But when we reached the immense portico that leads to the garden vista, we found the great doors shut and padlocked with one of those colossal mediae-val padlocks and chains so common in India. There was nothing for it but to peep through a crack which afforded only a kind of mouse-eye view of a fraction of the white dome, gleaming softly in the moonlight.

Feeling rather foolish, we drove back to the hotel. I had been suffering from a sore eye, and before getting into bed I groped still half-asleep for the eye ointment that I had put on the dressing-table. A second later I uttered such a ghastly yell that poor Stuart nearly fell out of bed, and berated me soundly. As if it hadn't been enough going on a wild goose chase in the middle of the night, I had inadvertently squeezed a good dollop of sun tan cream into my eye : I had no idea it could sting so painfully. When he grasped what had happened he forgave me for the fearful din I'd made; and we slept again at last.

Fatehpur Sikri near Agra—Akbar's deserted red citadel nearly seven miles in circumference, occupied for only fifteen years, is quite fascinating. Problems of water supply and of health conditions soon made it unihabitable, and Akbar returned to Agra. His summer bed at Fatehpur Sikri is an enormous block of stone, built about ten feet above a shallow flooring that was flooded to keep him cool in the hot season—a kind of early air-conditioning. This curious bedroom had inner passage-ways by which he could visit the houses of his various ladies without being observed— Miriam's house, the Turkish Queen's house, and other palaces and even offices. His giant open-air checkerboard also stirred the imagination, for he played checkers in a suitably grand manner— with slave girls for pieces.

I sat on the top of a lovely building, the Ankh Michauli, in which rather romantically the Emperor is said to have played hide and seek with his ladies, but which in fact had some quite prosaic use. Here we managed to shake off the pestiferous young guide who had attached himself to us, after fighting for the honour with another equally unpleasant type, and for a short while we had peace in which to enjoy Akbar's strange red city. Our roof top was close to the Diwan-i-Khas, and overlooking the long five-storeyed building of the Panch Mahal (*panch* meaning five, *mahal* meaning precious), with its piers and open colonnades, each storey stepped back from the other until only a small pavilion crowns the building. It was once a pleasure resort for the ladies of the harem.

The Diwan-i-Khas is most attractive, the octagonal private audience hall where Akbar sat on the top of a carved central pillar, reached by four narrow radiating balconies. His four ministers sat one at each corner, while his friends and advisers disputed in the hall below. That central pillar must have been perfect for Akbar's ego—although it is rather doubtful if the ego of a man such as he ever needed boosting.

In the forts and palaces of Agra the sudden, vivid appearances of lively Indian women and girls, brought a note of brilliance and colour to the deserted stone; as grouping themselves on little balconies, emerging suddenly, floatingly from narrow passages in the wall's thickness, they seemed to pose gracefully, their saris streaming in the cool breeze high above the river on some turret, or dangerously low-walled balcony.

In New Delhi there was some business to be done; visa hunting

again, and Ark had to be serviced, so on the first opportunity we
called at the Iranian Embassy, and heard with sinking hearts that
the Consul was in Kashmir, delayed by bad weather—a situation
shaping ominously after the Calcutta pattern. We eventually left
our passports and completed forms, and were told to return on
the following day. We were informed that it was quite impossible
to grant *me* a visa, as I was described as a writer. The Consul was
still detained in Kashmir. Another day passed, and Stuart returned yet again; this time the Consul had arrived. It was now
perfectly in order for me to have a visa, but on no account could
Stuart have one, because not only was he described as a Government servant, but also Bahrein appeared in his passport. If this
were eliminated, and a letter produced from the British Consul
describing Stuart as a *retired* Government servant the matter
might be solved. Stuart went to the British Embassy, got his letter,
had the offending Bahrein duly erased and rushed back—only to
find the Iranian Consulate closed for the day. At the hotel he
walked up and down our room, cursing gently : 'I'd like to cas-
trate the ruddy lot !' he finished up—on a note of such righteous
fury that both he and I had to burst out laughing.

On the fourth morning he returned once more and after a prolonged wait was told to fill in a fresh application form. At last he
was called into the Consul's presence; for an appreciable time
there was silence while the Consul examined the British Embassy
letter, and the newly-written application form. Eventually he
said : 'The form is not correct.'

'What do you mean, exactly?' asked Stuart.

'It says—"Government servant *retired*". It is wrong.'

'But that was what you wanted. . . .'

'It should be—"retired Government servant"—I cannot give
you the visa !'

'May the words be reversed? It means the same—' Stuart
pointed out gently.

'No, it is impossible. I can *not* grant you a visa . . . !' An empha-
tic statement, which sounded alarmingly final. This was a blow.
We *must* travel through Persia, there was no other overland way;
and besides that the blue mosques of Isfahan were one of the
journey's objectives. The only alternative to Persia, would be to
ship from Karachi to Iraq, a proposition neither of us welcomed.
In that moment all our hopes and careful plans appeared to be

dashed. But Stuart is a determined man, and has his own methods. He merely sat on where he was in dead silence; while the Consul ignoring him, wrote out a single letter three times very slowly, and very slowly tore up each one.

So the minutes ticked by : it was nearly lunch time. *Something* was bound to happen—Stuart consoled himself that at least he had not been thrown out.

At the end of an hour exactly, the Consul raised his head. Stuart had won the silent battle.

'All right. You reverse the words on the form, and I'll grant you the visa.' The statement was made without a smile, or any change of expression.

Early on the fourth day while we were still waiting for the visas, we went to meet Mr Nehru. This had been arranged through the good offices of the Indian Press Attaché, who had received a message about us from his colleague in Rangoon. Every morning, or nearly every morning Mr Nehru holds an informal early session during which he meets and mingles with all manner of people.

We were received by a grey-haired Indian lady, her warm and friendly manner became even more so when we mentioned Lady Louis. She turned then, with sadness in her brown eyes. 'Oh !' she sighed, '—and she was here with us only a few weeks ago—Come and see the rooms she had !'

We followed her through reception rooms—so crowded with waiting visitors, that there was scarcely space to squeeze through the doors—and along a passage and into a little suite, simple but charming, giving onto a wide sun-drenched flower-banked garden beyond. We stood in silence for a moment, thinking of that amazing personality whom we mourned. Then our hostess said : 'She was our *very* best house guest—we shall never forget her. . . .'

We went out into the garden then, grateful for the pleasant warmth of the sun. Opening onto this garden was a long verandah room crowded with peasants sitting on the floor; tall, beturbaned servants went around swiftly among them, handing trays of cakes and tea under the seraphic gaze of heavenly apsaras, photographed in temples such as Khajuraoh. Mr Nehru presently came out onto the verandah : all the people stood up with a sudden clattering of teacups, and pressing their hands together in the *namaskar* they bowed in greeting; he moved among them smilingly.

Eagerly and naturally they stretched out their hands to garland him with roses and marigolds.

After some minutes we ourselves were presented, and he spoke briefly with us. He is shorter than I had somehow been led to expect, and the limpness of his handshake came as a surprise in a man of so much power, but his good looks are still remarkable. As he questioned us in his soft hesitant voice, his handsome eyes flying a little, I received the extraordinary impression that this great and distinguished man was shy—perhaps not shy, but remote and lonely.

In the garden the people, rich and poor, followed him everywhere, he was like the Pied Piper, moving smiling and quiet between brilliant flower beds, across impeccable lawns; here and there he would pause to speak a word or two, and to be garlanded afresh.

The most impressive thing about that sunny morning interlude was the universal look of deep devotion on the faces of the people present—the men, women and children gathered there. It was all over in half an hour; and at nine o'clock punctutally he retreated to his office.

❋ 7 ❋

Landslide in Kashmir: on to Amritsar

It was pleasant to be out in the country once more, leaving New Delhi for Kashmir. The road at first was good and straight. The sugar-cane was still being harvested; there were women with immensely full petticoats that swirled provocatively around their ankles as they walked; there were young Sikhs with alert, fresh faces, and tall brown men and pale-coloured proud camels at little oases of trees around Persian water-wheels. Then suddenly the landscape opened out and snowy hills appeared beyond.

I think this day was perhaps the beginning of the real change for us both : we were enjoying ourselves, on the move again, going constantly further away, and with the possibly dangerous part of the journey in Baluchistan and Persia as a challenge to come.

We resolved from then on to stop at little Dak bungalows or if possible Circuit houses; we had had quite enough of hotels.

We slept that night in our first Dak bungalow at a little place called Dasuya. The khanasama, who seemed amazed to see us, was an immensely tall man resembling a nervous, under-fed horse; he had a few words of English. We camped in a small bare bedroom, and when we had bathed, dipper fashion, the khanasama rather apologetically set before us two piping hot dishes, one of plain rice and another of dahl and onions; it was the simplest of meals but hot and fresh and, being very hungry we enjoyed it. We both felt much happier than we had in Delhi. Despite the peasant fare, the small bare room, the leaking 'thunder-boxes' and aged tin chamber-pot in the bathroom, somehow it was more enjoyable than the so-called luxury hotel at five guineas a head a day.

Before we slept we heard the khanasama and a friend settling down, unasked on the verandah outside our door to guard Ark.

In the morning, uncertain what to pay, Stuart handed over the official Dak bungalow rental fee, and five rupees for the food and service. 'Is that all right?' he asked.

'Sahib, I have *too* much money!' The khanasama's huge sunken eyes rolled a little and his sad gaunt face broke into a wide and friendy grin.

Again and again in these little old-fashioned places, relics of a past era, we received this surprising and happy impression, that as English people we were really welcome.

In the morning we were away soon after seven o'clock, a blue Krishna bird toccing busily overhead swooped almost into Ark's roof as we drove back towards the main road. A good omen, but again the electrical fault began to give trouble. The road deteriorated rapidly, bucking and swooping like the waves of the sea, and once or twice taken unawares I hit the roof, but one soon learns how to sit tight on this kind of surface. We were in the Punjab now, and notices appeared written in the familiar Arabic script. At a check-post on the India Kashmir border we met a friendly ex-naval artificer, he wished us luck on the drive up to Srinagar, but his news of the road ahead was not encouraging.

After this border, extensive road reconstruction and several lengthy diversions over vast, dry river beds delayed our progress considerably. Some of these diversions were as much as a mile long, sandy, wild and stony, fit settings for the camels that so sedately trod them. Snow mountains now showed again ahead and after passing Jammu, with its high-set fort and wide moraine-like country, the road began to climb in earnest. At one point, we noticed a man asleep on a narrow ledge despite a sheer drop below to a river gorge, and marvelled; was it madness, or lack of imagination? It was almost as crazy as the boy we had seen cycling in one of Delhi's most crowded streets, reading a book as he went.

The hills seemed to cradle the road, rising like giant fangs all around us. At two police posts we were offered cups of tea, and there were pressing invitations to stay and talk. At a third post again we were stopped, but not this time for tea. Here the police said that the road to the Banihal Pass beyond Batote had fallen in, and that we could not be permitted to continue as Batote was already crowded out, and no food or accommodation remained. But when they saw that we had our own supplies and could sleep in the van we were eventually allowed to go on.

The scenery grew more and more magnificent as the road

wound up into the hills towards Patou Pass at 6,000 feet above sea-level. Beyond Patou we dropped down a little through a dark coniferous forest to the tiny alpine village of Batote—merely a string of houses clinging to the ravine's edge, it recalled the Haute Savoie above Martigny.

As we turned the last bend towards it a depressing sight confronted us: a long line of trucks stood nose to tail vanishing in perspective around the shoulder of the mountain. These trucks, of the kind seen everywhere in India known as public carriers—though like the English public school they are all private—invariably have, as I have previously mentioned, 'Horn Please' or 'Horn Pleas' written on the rear in large letters. But it was no earthly use horning this lot, they were well and truly stuck. I counted 105 of them in the village alone, and it was said that there were 200 more beyond stretching up to the landslide, and another 200 on the far side.

At the Batote village check post we learned that the road *might* be opened on the following day, or *'almost* certainly' on the day after. The Rest-house was full of course to capacity. We decided to try and find a flat space, not easy in a mountain village—so that we might sleep comfortably in Ark. By luck we took a wrong turning and drew up sharply on a narrow terrace outside a small Forestry Department Office. Several faces appeared at windows above: Stuart explained our mistake, and we were at once invited to stay on the little terrace, a few feet above the line of trucks.

Darkness soon fell. We had cooked our supper and washed up, I had done a little work and we were beginning to think about settling down to sleep when seven men arrived out of the black night. They were friendly visitors, led by an amiable Syed, a judge returning from duties in the plains to his home in Srinagar; he had come to offer the use of his bathroom in the Resthouse for morning ablutions. They gathered round in the warm lamp-light, and started firing off questions. The Judge then came into Ark, sat down on the bed beside me and began to cross-examine me about my work. Although several of them had been marooned already for a day or two they were extremely cheerful and philosophical, and there was plenty of laughter. The Judge said that he intended walking across the landslide—it was twenty-two yards wide—if the road were not cleared on the following day. He would telephone for a car to be sent from Srinagar to pick him up. It was maddening to think that it was only the length of a cricket pitch that stood between us and the Bannihal Pass.

Below our small terrace was the caravanserai of truck drivers, they were mostly Sikhs, a rather handsome lot. One little bar was open, and a few tiny shops. The drivers had made camp-fires all along the roadside, the light flickered up, and with it the noise of their talk, the smell of wood fire smoke, of ghee, chapatties and dahl.

When at last our jovial visitors left, we began to settle in for the night. Optimistically Stuart decided to sleep on the wooden verandah of the Forestry Office : the idea being to awake in the morning to the glorious sight of the high snows. I wished very much that I were half as brave as he, but it was too cold and damp for me outside and so I settled down comfortably in Ark.

I awoke to a streaming morning : now even the near mountains were hidden in rain. I looked out and saw that Stuart was still fast asleep and more or less dry. In the little bar below a big fire blazed; the drivers, huddled in blankets and great coats were walking disconsolately up and down beside the long row of rain-soaked and immobile 'public carriers'.

At the Resthouse later, we heard from the Syed that a message had just come through; night-long rain had cause fresh earth falls and it would now be three, or more likely four days before the road could be cleared. So much worse was it that he had now abandoned the idea of walking across the landslide. After a short confabulation, Stuart and I decided that we could not delay four days or possibly more, and reluctantly agreed that the only thing to do was to return to the plains.

We descended upon Jammu towards evening. Owing to the rough roads the loose electrical connection had again begun to give trouble, and it was getting late. But despite the risk we pushed on into the rapidly darkening night, again traversing the barren lands of lower Kashmir, and those eight long dark dry river beds, now a little fearfully, hoping we should not lose our way in their wide sandy tracks, and uncertain where we might camp, or put up for the night in this desolate place.

But we were in luck : the young Indian ex-naval man whom we had met before was again on duty at the frontier check post, and he volunteered to guide us to a Resthouse in Madhopur a few miles further on. This proved to be an excellent old-style Government building, a Circuit House and not normally for the use of tourists. But luckily it was empty and he readily obtained permission for us to sleep there. The Khanasama was off duty; there was no bedding, nor was there any running water in the large bathroom. But none of this worried us : I soon made up our beds in the high ceilinged suite, while Stuart warmed our humble stew on the verandah. We felt very snug, the Ark safely close at hand in a garden full of roses, sweet peas and deep blue cornflowers; and we were lulled by the sound of unseen rushing waters.

Stuart poured two glasses of Indian whisky and as the stew began to bubble in the pot we sat by the fire for a few moments, savouring the odd contrast of these spacious surroundings with our present nomadic ways.

'I think we might call ourselves Nomadic Brits now,' he said. A classification which would look well, perhaps, on future passports or on those Consulate forms, but I doubted if it would be any better received than 'Government servant retired'.

In the morning the tone completely changed; Nomadic Brit reverted once more to 'Sahib' and 'Memsahib', for the khanasama had returned. Early morning tea was served, hot and cold water ran in the bathroom, and soon we were breakfasting on fresh fruit and fried eggs served in a vast dining-room next to our suite.

From Madhopur, the great Sikh leader, Ranjit Singh, built a canal to carry the turbulent River Ravi to the Golden Temple in the Pool of Nectar—Amritsar. As we breakfasted we listened to the sound of the waters, it seemed louder all around the house, and now in the morning light we could see the canals and weirs and sluice gates. Our friends the green parakeets and the blue Krishna birds were already swooping across the flower-filled garden.

After breakfast we stopped at Pathankot to find a garage where the electrical fault might be put right. As usual, when there was a delay, I climbed into the back of the van to get on with some work. As I was banging away at my typewriter the customary little crowd gathered round—mostly young Sikh and Punjabi mechanics, friendly people as we found all Indians to be, and one of them spoke English. Unexpectedly, someone brought a tray of tea and set it on the table before me, and while I drank the tea we discussed stamps, flowers, photographs and exchanged addresses. When all was done, the speedometer back in place, the wire now firmly fixed, Stuart asked the cost — but this friendly garage would not take any payment.

Amritsar is the holy centre of Sikhism, and as we drove south towards it that day we saw an increasing number of Sikhs, many armed in the traditional manner with large swords. The Muslim people were colourfully dressed, for they were already beginning to celebrate the end of Ramadan. Picturesque creaking wooden ferris wheels had been set up for the children in many towns, and in several places there were some curious processions — heavily veiled figures riding white ponies. At first we thought they were brides going to a wedding feast, but soon I noticed something odd about them; they all had large feet shod in black leather shoes — strangely enough they were not brides at all, but bridegrooms going to the nuptial house. They wore light garments and were so heavily veiled — with elaborate, woven, and embroidered tassels — very much like the fringes that the caparisoned ponies themselves wore to keep the flies out of their eyes — that is was impossible to guess their sex until one noticed the tell-tale feet.

This, the beginning of the great Indus valley system, watered by the Ravi canal, was a far greener countryside than any we had yet seen in India. The wheat fields were bigger and the crops heavier; and countless Persian water-wheels were creaking rhythmically, the falling water glittering in the little islands of their shade trees.

Trying to find the Golden Temple in Amritsar we soon lost our way, but once again a helpful man appeared at the crucial moment as we hesitated in the melée. A young Sikh on a bicycle drew alongside the van and called out breathlessly above the street hubbub: 'I'm from the tourist agency! — I saw your car, and I *dashed* to that place — but missed you . . . *I* will lead you to the Golden Temple!'

It was all that we could do to keep pace with him as he wormed his way rapidly through crowded streets, under the deep archway of the old city, past a garlanded white marble statue of Queen Victoria — and eventually through a crazily narrow so-called one-way but apparently all-ways lane to the outer walls of this Sikh holiest of holies.

In an office in the walls we had to sign a register: under the heading of 'occupation' Stuart, who had learnt some wariness after the experience in the Iranian Embassy, wrote simply one word — 'man'. The burly young Sikh in charge was amused. He clapped his hands, and roared his appreciation in a deep robust voice. Apparently Stuart could not have chosen a better description, he was congratulated — 'to be a real man', the Sikh said, 'was the true aim of all Sikhs, the warrior people of India.'*

We were then equipped with woollen socks, and Stuart had to bind his head in a duster in lieu of a turban, as he was now growing a beard his appearance was a little wild, and the bright yellow duster enhanced it. I looked scarcely more respectable, very sunburnt and my hair tied in a red Benares scarf.

So we began shuffling round the wide marble terrace in the wake of an appalling guide. Fortunately for me, I was so overwhelmed by what I saw that I hardly listened to a word he said and he fastened his unwanted attentions firmly upon Stuart who was forced to listen, and who in consequence now looks back on that crowded hour in a very different light.

Perhaps it was partly our piratical appearance that accounted for the mobs of people, they were not beggars, who dogged every step we took. There was no room to turn round or even to pause without actually standing on someone's toes. The mob, although determined it seemed to the point of fanaticism to stick to us wherever we went was mercifully as nothing compared to the swarm of flies massed on and above that superb terrace.† But for me not even this hemming in by the mob, nor the flies, nor the shattering remarks made by the guide in *Cockney* could spoil the beauty of the temple in the amber light of sunset.

The 'Pool of Nectar' — Amritsar itself, once a secluded spot in the forest, is now a marble enclosed tank, 510 feet square. In the centre, rising ephemerally from the water, the temple gleamed fabulously golden in the westering sunlight.

I could not take my eyes off it, the effect was astounding, a dream of sheer oriental splendour. Its lines are simple, it is almost square, a serene pavilion of marble, pietra dura and gilt, apparently floating on the surface of the great tank, for only a single long slender causeway on the eastern side links it with the marble terrace.

* Guru Nanak (1469-1538) said that 'Man becomes man when the Ultimate Truth dawns on him, when he can love truth sincerely.'
† Baal Zebub could really have lorded it here. See footnote page 169.

The guide dragged Stuart off to look at a mural of some famous warrior whose name eludes me, who went on fighting after his head was cut off; and then dragged him back again to watch the 'silman and 'oly scarp' as he called salmon and carp in his unlikely Cockney twang. I wanted only to feast my eyes on that pavilion, I should probably never see it again as it appeared now, I must content myself with this one gilded vision, the temple aglow against a sky of cerulean blue.

The flies and gnats swarming everywhere seemed especially to congregate under some rather beautiful aged plum trees, said to cure leprosy, and the urchins buzzed around as eagerly as the flies. One pretty little girl in such a hurry to join the crowd cannoned into Stuart all but knocking him down. The guide put a hand on her head, patted it unctuously, and said: 'Would yer like to tike a little student to England . . .?'

In the tank the ' 'oly scarp' rose languidly to the surface every now and again, disturbing the floating flowers with their ponderous wake.

Passing up and down the narrow causeway with their beturbaned menfolk was a never-ending stream of beautifully dressed Sikh women, in their voluminous trousers and light veils they were like a ripple of curving waves drifting to and from the golden shrine.

The four doors of the temple are open always to anyone who cares to enter, as a symbol of the anti-caste teaching of early Sikh gurus; men who had encouraged even the Shudra, lowest caste of all, to write songs and hymns that now appear in what the guide called 'the sicred book'. Again here, as at Khajuraoh, was a bas-relief of the 'Churning of the Sea of Milk' legend, the same that is so strongly and repeatedly represented at Angkor. I have often wondered if this can be a parallel to, or even the same as, the legend of Venus rising from the sea.

The sacred book of Sikhism, the Granth Sahib lay in the shrine, surrounded by flowers; people passing by on either side threw gifts of money before it. Musicians were playing and chanting, as the guide said: 'Sicred music they are 'aving all diy, drums and 'armoniums, pliying 'ighteen hours a diy—yer see. . . .'

As we left the terrace the sun was setting, turning the gilt and copper to bronze. We retrieved our shoes, took a warm farewell of the robust custodian and made our bewildered way back through the crowded lanes, the Malls and Charing Crosses, to our little hotel.

We were sorry that this was for us the last of India, the time had gone all too quickly. It was now March 28th, and we had to push on into Pakistan. After the experiences in Calcutta, we were not looking forward to the Indian Customs, so at Atari, while Stuart went to deal with frontier formalities, I resigned myself to a long wait and retreated into the back of Ark to work. But almost at once a smiling face appeared at the door.

Some of the conversations I had thus on the journey were illuminating, it is surprising how easily people seemed to expand in this manner. The talk that morning was on Hindu beliefs and mythology with a man who was interested in art and religion. He was one of several Hindus who have before and since then, told me frankly that they themselves could not really understand Hinduism. 'Some people,' he said with a smile, '— laugh at Ganesh . . .'

I assured him that I was not among them; Ganesh is one of my favourites. He asked me about my work; and when I told him he smiled again and said it was good, for : ' "an unambitious wife means a lazy husband" — Work is a moral necessity,' he added; '— each day has but eighty-six thousand four hundred seconds !'

'They've gone all too quickly for me, in India !' I replied, and meant what I said.

To our surprise, the frontier formalities took little over half an hour; Stuart soon returned and we drove away from India through a garden full of roses. I felt there was more than a hint of symbolism in this no man's land of roses that, with its blood-red flowers and thorns divided two countries which should be one.

As we left India, like a farewell gesture the shadow of her flag played briefly across Ark's windows, waving gently in the brilliant sunlight.

8

Pakistan and a Sandstorm

By 'the Lion's Roar', Kim's great brass cannon in Lahore city, there is a signpost that points to—'London—6372 miles'.

This made England seem suddenly much nearer but by our route it was still considerably further away than that.

I liked Lahore at once: it was en fête for the end of Ramadan, 'Id as it is called in Pakistan. A pretty town, sunny and gay; people were dashing along the Mall in pony carts, to the zoological gardens, to the mosques, or out visiting, walking in wide tree-bordered streets, and cool avenues of checkered shade. Instead of five-foot ways there were large striped awnings outside the shops; the names of the shopkeepers had an Arabian ring about them, here Sinbads, Aladdins and Ali Babas were as common as Jones and Smith in England.

Due to the 'Id holidays we could neither post our letters, because we couldn't buy stamps, nor obtain our mail from the A.A. offices because the peon who had the keys was away fishing. But an obliging A.A. official had Ark serviced and washed; and was himself a mine of useful information as to the road ahead, and the hazards of the Lorelai route to Quetta in particular. Despite many travellers' letters, and local advice, the London A.A. has persistently advocated this route over a period of years. Not only is the surface appalling and in parts broken away, the Lahore official said, but wandering Afghans were a menace. He strongly recommended taking the longer but safer route to the south, via Sukkur and Jacobabad. He had often travelled in Persia, we noticed the Persian contact is strong in this part of Pakistan, and he also had advice to give on Persia, and an address or two in case we needed it.

While we waited for the A.A. peon to return from his fishing holiday so that we might have our letters, we wandered round Lahore a little. We walked in the Gardens, listened to the red-coated clearly British-trained band, and watched the crowds;

men, and veiled girls and half-veiled women wandering among the flowers as the young *'Id* moon rose, and excited boys in pink shirts and ear-rings who ran dancing to the music.

We tried to find the tomb of the tragic Anarkali but could not get inside the compound. She was the 'Pomegranate Blossom' of Akbar's harem, but unfortunately she was loved also by Salim, Akbar's son. According to my Handbook, it was said that as a punishment for Salim's smile 'she was buried alive, and the pathetic distich engraved on her sarcophagus certainly indicates that Salim was her lover:

' "Ah, if I could see again the face of my beloved,

To the day of judgement would I give thanks to my Creator." '

'Id finished, we were at last able to leave Lahore on March 31st, but we had driven only eight miles when a nail in a tyre caused fresh delay, and by midday we were back again in the hotel sitting in the 'Permit Room' (the bar), frustratedly sipping Pakistani gin and tonic while the tyre was being mended. Fortunately we had only about 125 miles to go to Montgomery where we had planned to stay the night in order to visit Harappa, ancient city of the lost Indus civilization.

This canal country on the edge of the Great Indian Desert was attractive, its casuarinas made me think of Trengganu, but the land was so utterly flat and the skies so cloudless that it seemed sometimes as if we were driving over the very edge of the world.

Montgomery's decidedly English atmosphere, a legacy from the past, was a pronounced contrast. We went to a Canal Resthouse in a wide flowery garden, to ask permission to sleep there, and were directed to the house of a young Pakistani executive engineer across the tree-shaded road. He seemed eager to talk, and I noticed that he had a number of English books. He spoke with obvious pride of the Indus irrigation scheme, and of how the desert really had blossomed like the rose, and to a certain extent he hinted that he missed the British influence; perhaps he wished to flatter—I do not know—but his manner was sincere.

As we were talking I saw a car drive up, a woman heavily veiled in a *burkha* sat inside. He went away for a moment: presently he returned and said to me apologetically: 'You know we have a very strange custom here—purdah. My wife would like to meet you, but she can't come in, because the company's mixed. Would you mind . . .?'

He went towards some thick curtains at one side of the room, I followed him out into a passage, and behind the arras, as it were, I was introduced to his wife who stood there waiting. She was quite young, a pretty, smiling woman, now unveiled. There was nothing I could do but to shake hands and smile back, for neither of us could speak more than a word or two of the other's tongue. After a little while I retreated to the men, wondering that such strict purdah could still exist among people so obviously modern, young and alert. What would she do if she were to be transferred with him to Karachi—for instance—would she change her ways, or would family disapproval be too strong?

As it happened, the Canal Resthouse was occupied by a judge on tour, so the engineer sent us on, with a bearer to act as guide, to another smaller Canal Resthouse at a little place called Ballewalla.

We arrived after sunset in a half-flooded garden full of flowers. The khanasama; a born comedian, a man of oddly staccato movements; bounced about, comically bewildered but eager to oblige. As swift as the parakeets he raced across the garden to place long chairs for us on a kind of central terrace, raised above the flood water, where it was easy to guess it had been the habit of former Britishers to sit at dusk and drink their chota-pegs. At the double he brought water and glasses, and Stuart fetched whisky from Ark. It was beautiful in that garden of flowers and mirrored sky, the young moon rising brilliant above dusky trees; the trees were dark against the still fiery west, the road was marked by a distant cloud of luminous dust against which sometimes a frieze of figures walked like people in a shadow play.

Soon it was quite dark and we went inside to ask for 'garam pani'—hot water—one of our few expressions. The over-anxious khanasama galloped about with steaming pails, and presently brought his wife and child to watch as we made up our camp beds and cooked supper.

When we had cleared away the supper things, the khanasama bounded in again; whipped off his turban, used it with histrionic vigour to wipe the table clean and promptly replaced it on his head.

Later, as we were brewing tea he reappeared with two young men, one of whom said that he spoke English. A tremendous conversation then ensued in very broken English, until in despair the

khanasama seized Stuart by the arm and we all swayed out
volubly onto the verandah. Then the khanasama flung himself
down suddenly and violently, full length on the flagstones—
clearly he wished to sleep on guard. His clownish dumb-crambo
was so comic that I hardly knew how to keep a straight face.
Stuart did his best to say that it was not necessary, and we attempted a retreat towards bed. But all three men followed persistently into our room, still arguing loudly but incomprehensibly,
and still looking bewildered. Stuart suggested to me that I should
begin to make movements as if I were about to undress, but this
seemed only to delay matters further, and finally he had to eject
the men gently but firmly. We quickly closed the doors and shutters, and went to bed at last, feeling weak with suppressed
laughter and not a little bewildered ourselves.

But the night was all too short; soon after four a.m. we were
awoken by loud bangs and yells, a rattling of the numerous doors
and shutters, and the urgent voice of that irrepressible khanasama
respectfully shouting: *'Sahib-ji, sahib-ji—garam pani, garam
pani!'*

Stuart staggered up sleepily and managed to indicate by some
fantastic mime: '— not until the birds start flying—for God's
sake!'

It was the first day of summer, which perhaps accounted for
that very early call; on that day the whole of Pakistan's official
routine switches to a summer timetable, offices open earlier and
close for an afternoon siesta. It was a glorious morning, and when
we had taken farewell of our perturbed khanasama, who must
have been thankful to see the last of us, we drove the few miles to
Harappa. With Mohenjodara, Harappa is part of the ancient
Indus civilization, something of a mystery, one of the greatest
nameless kingdoms of western Asia dating from 2500 to 1500
B.C. It once lay on the banks of the River Ravi, which has
changed its course. Its ancient people were agriculturists, as is
known by their beautiful circular corn-pounding platforms made
of radiating bricks, looking today almost as if new, and also from
the remains of their granaries. They laid out their city neatly in
rows of houses for workers, governors and merchants, 'marshalled,
like a military cantonment in a way that bespeaks authority.'

We had the whole place to ourselves. The quietness and the
sunbaked loneliness of the site were impressive; a wonderful sense

of timelessness assailed us, linking this ancient past to our brief day.

A one-roomed Resthouse has been built at the site in a garden of roses and petunias, and in a little museum attached were many fascinating objects taken from the excavations. There were toy waggons, some five thousand years old and yet identical with those of the Punjab today; and terra-cotta 'whistling birds' such as my own children played with; small figurines, coins, scaled weights, and gamesmen and tiny soapstone seals, finely cut with Brahminy bulls, and other animals, figures or designs, and with the pictographic script that still today baffles all attempts to decipher it. It remains unique, has no affinity with any other known script, and is without known descendants. So Harappa is a mystery : it was perhaps part of a civilization that was wiped out by some sudden catastrophe, possibly the flooding of the Indus.

The small things intrigued me most for their delicacy; but some of the tiny figurines were crudely made by building up of the clay—even to the eyes and little pointed breasts; not exactly by modelling and shaping, but as a child today begins to make its plasticene figures. There were bigger relics too, huge mortars, bath jars, heaters, even flat irons of terra-cotta, and beautiful black-patterned *kalasas*—the long-necked water jars.

From Harappa we drove on to Panchnad, the 'Five Rivers', where five great rivers flowing down from the Himalayas meet above their conflux with the Indus herself.

The land was flat but where the canals irrigated it, orange trees and wheat fields flourished, there were patches too of some bright green fodder crop, and the precious water glittering in the sunlight fell from the innumerable buckets of countless Persian wells.

On the narrow road, dashing-looking men on horseback trotted gaily along, theatrically romantic as if they had stepped out of a more decorative and much earlier age than ours.

That day we encountered our first Afghans on the march from winter camps in the plains to summer pastures in the mountains—a superb sight. We were witnessing a part of the ancient biannual migration of the herds, the custom of transhumance, and we were fortunate to see, later, a similar migration of the Kurds on the Mediterranean Fertile Crescent side of these vast uplands.

Great congeries of golden camels went swaying along in the tree shade to the clunk-clink of their strings of bells. A few donkeys, or sometimes just one small donkey always leads the camel train.* Everything is piled atop the animals, charpoy beds, tents, cocks and hens, goats and kids, new-born woolly lambs, and lovely children with dusky faces and rose-red cheeks, their dark tousled heads nodding to the camel's stride. Baby camels trotted beside their mothers with a nervous springy gait, their thick flocculent coats woolly and ochre-brown like koala bears. We soon had evidence of the 'predatory hands' of the nomads, as Baedeker so aptly decribes those of the Kurds, even tiny children would stretch out a grimy paw as if automatically towards a passing car, though it might be several yards away.

We moved past these wonderful caravans all day; there were beautiful unveiled girls with mocking dark eyes; arrogant swashbuckling and magnificent young men, aged patriarchs, striding boisterous women, and in the wake of the camels the noisy, scrambling herds, bucking through the dust clouds.

The sight of these people on the move was one of the most splendid things that we saw on the trek, and we count ourselves lucky to have hit the migratory season. But perhaps it was not so much luck as judgment, for it was the correct time to travel; a time we had picked with care although, as it so happened, quite independently of age-old transhumant lore.

The friendly engineer at Montgomery had advised against stopping at Multan—famed for dust, heat, beggars and cemeteries—and had armed us with a letter to a colleague at Panchnad, where we hoped we might again sleep at a Canal Resthouse.

Nearing Panchnad at about six in the evening we were held up at the Abbasia Canal bridge for General Ayub Khan's first minister who was about to cross. I climbed on top of Ark where I had a splendid view of the people and the herds likewise delayed. Below me was a group of women crouching on a cotton carpet, they wore the Pakistani *burkha*, unhappy, drooping figures, peering and peeping through their meshed eye-holes like so many white spectres, while the young men wandered around affectionately and uninhibitedly entangled—perhaps it is small wonder that the youths behave like that when their women folk look like nothing but a pack of ghosts, or an enclosed order of faceless nuns.

* This is the invariable custom throughout the East, for what reason I do not know, unless it be, as Stuart insists, simply because a donkey's eyes are closer to the ground.

Chandel dynasty temple at Khajuraoh, Madhya Pradesh

Ganesh, the elephant-headed son of Siva, on a temple at Khajuraoh

An apsara in the outdoor museum at Khajuraoh

Besides Ark there was only one other car, a broken-down taxi, but there were several bus-loads of people; forty or fifty camels and their tall, bold-eyed flower-sniffing Afghan herdsmen, Afghan women and children, and a lovely bright-eyed girl with a curved knife stuck in her turban. There was a herd of cows, another of sheep, a few trucks, the usual itching of urchins, some farmers playing drums and a trumpet; and one wildly abandoned young man—who more amorous than all the rest behaved like some crazy wanton, repeatedly flinging himself upon his laughing, staggering male friends, using both arms and legs in clinging embrace.

The camels looked bored and slightly indignant as they always do. I could not, of course, see how the purdah women looked, but from their attitudes it was clear that they were pretty bored too, if unfortunately less indignant than the camels.

I made several futile attempts to draw the Afghan herdsmen, magnificent in loose falling black turbans, voluminous trousers, and full-sleeved coloured shirts under short bolero-like waistcoats. But whatever I did to disguise the fact that I was drawing them, these hawk-eyed handsome devils invariably spotted it, and I think for the first time (as an artist) I was well and truly outstared. Their laughing eyes spoke so frank a challenge that I was unable to endure it : they were too much for me, and I had to give up the attempt. It was a pity for they were splendid; tall, lean, bursting with health and *élan*. The flowers that they always carried between their thin smiling lips, or twirled below their nostrils, seemed not to detract from, but rather to stress their overwhelming masculinity; and their blatant scorn for the antics of the homosexual was clear for all to read.

At dusk, a devout old man began to say his prayers under an acacia tree. It was beginning to get cold, then at last after a wait of nearly two hours, and several false alarms, the General's minister eventually arrived. We all stood up to wave and cheer, and he responded gaily amid the shouts, the herds' and the camel bells. So it was quite dark by the time everyone began charging across the bridge.

On the far side we stopped to ask the way to the Canal Resthouse; a young English-speaking Pakistani ran up to help, and came into the van to guide us. The Resthouse was close at hand but he talked hard as if anxious to practise his English. When we asked what his work was he replied disarmingly cheerful : 'I am idle !'

F

We delivered our letter to the young engineer in charge; he insisted on giving us tea, and sent his bearer across to see the khanasama with instructions for an evening meal. It was a charming place, as are all these Canal Resthouses and engineers' quarters, secluded, shady and neat in gardens of English summer flowers. The khanasama, one of those long-legged, old-fashioned gaunt but kindly men, spoke a few words of English; and there was a three-day local *mela,* a religious fair in connection with the end of Ramadan, at a neighbouring village, so we were tempted to stay two nights—to catch up on work, clean out Ark, rest a little, and go to the fair. . . .

Two mornings later when we stopped to eat our breakfast some miles along the road, who should appear but the 'I am idle' boy; he rushed up beaming, like a long-lost friend, hands clasped high in greeting, and wished us a hearty 'good afternoon!'

There were flute-playing pedestrians on the road, more laden camels, some small carts with solid wheels exactly like the five-thousand-year-old terra-cotta model at Harappa, and—near the turning to the *mela,* we encountered an amiable dancing bear, who performed for us and who seemed, and I hope was, on happy terms with his master.

We had a three hundred mile drive before us that day, which for Ark on such roads is a long one, we never attempted to drive her fast over bad surfaces. We hoped to reach Nutal or possibly further before nightfall on the road to the Bolan Pass and Quetta.

In this part of Pakistan, the Sind, the summer heat is so great that trains run only at night. Even then (April 3rd), it was hot, with a furnace-like heat, especially when we had crossed the Indus on the Sukkur Barrage (4,725 feet long) and came into the fly-ridden, dusty oven of New Sukkur.

The grilling afternoon that followed was the only really uncomfortably hot one of the whole trek. The sun burnt with a fierceness I have never known—before or since, and after a while the passenger seat became almost unbearable. The true meaning of posh* was only too clear, we took it in turns to drive during that long afternoon in order to rest from the scorching rays on the port side; and we decided to put Ark into a sort of desert purdah as soon as we could buy some suitable material in Quetta.

We hurried through Jacobabad, wondering what on earth it

* 'Port out and starboard home.'

could be like in that remote outpost in May and June. General Jacob must have been among the hardiest of Britishers; for in this area early summer shade temperatures of 127 degrees Fahrenheit are known, while in the winter 22 to 23 degrees of frost occur. . . .

It was getting late; we were tired and hungry. The afternoon was forbidding; the wild-looking Afghans were still on the march; ahead the plain stretched away to distant, dark mountains, over which a storm was brewing.

The map showed a small Resthouse at Nutal, then still some miles ahead. We reached this little place at sunset; it was nothing more than a few mud huts. Groups of Afghans were now already camped here and there for the night with their camel trains. We too wanted to stop; we had hoped after that long hot drive for a bath of sorts in this Nutal Resthouse. However, no Resthouse was to be found; a man directed us 'further on', but we saw nothing but a group of ruined railway buildings. The storm was rolling down from the mountains, so we stopped where we were in the middle of the track; cooked up a hasty supper of soup, and broached our one reserve bottle of Hennessey, while the lightning ahead zig-zagged in gorgeous but ominous flashes of purple and lilac, and in the distance sand began to rise on the wind.

Stuart was hurriedly packing away the cooking gear, when I saw the first sand cloud tearing over the plain towards us. We slammed the side door to, jumped into the front together, shut all the windows and waited in awed silence for the onslaught.

It came frighteningly, soundless on the heels of the vacuum before it; sweeping up in great tongues of brown sand, like flames, with the power of a tidal wave.

The Ark is tall and we had no idea how much force she could stand without toppling over. It was an almost exhilarating moment of tingling fear. We sat huddled together well to windward, waiting for the impact.

Then, as the storm hit her, Ark rocked violently, and the sound broke with a sudden rushing of wind and a sharp slapping and buffeting of sand as hard as hailstones. We were completely enveloped in this rushing, blinding brown darkness that blotted out everything.

Still clutching each other and hoping our weight would keep Ark from going over, we watched breathlessly for a gap in the dense flying sand, and it seemed a long time before it came at last—a silvery, cold gleam of light.

Then, as the darkness lifted we saw that the windscreen, and half the van was coated thick with rain-clotted sand lying solid like great snow flakes on the glass and on all windward surfaces.

The storm centre was still black ahead; so rather shaken by our first sandstorm, and uncertain of ourselves, we decided to turn back to the mud huts of Nutal. Between the walls there we found some shelter from the wind. When its force had abated a little the owner of a small but undoubtedly bug-ridden pull-in for carmen nearby, came out to offer us beds. We declined, preferring to sleep in Ark, but presently he returned with a brass pitcher of water, cigarettes and a dish of hot chapatties. We felt snug now, more or less sheltered as we were by an angle of the mud walls and even enheartened by the attentions of the innkeeper—at least we were not alone in the wilderness. We ate the chapatties and drank some more of the brandy, and began to hope that we should now be more confident after our first rough encounter.

Above the howling of the wind outside, another knock came on the door, and once again the innkeeper put in his head : this time he had brought a small savoury omelette. While Stuart was paying him I saw that he looked hopefully at the Hennessey bottle on the table, and he began to say a whole lot of things which we could not understand but could guess at; and there was something too about a friend at the railway telegraph post.

After that we had some peace and were beginning to think of settling down for the night, when the man appeared yet again, this time bearing a letter in one hand, and a small glass containing a tot of something that looked like gin in the other. By signs he indicated that Stuart was to drink the gin, and let him have some of the Hennessey after which he so obviously lusted. Rather reluctantly Stuart exchanged glasses with him—the 'gin' being pretty raw alcohol—and we read the letter. Written on the back of a telegram form, it was evidently from the innkeeper's friend at the railway telegraph post. It was a little mystifying : 'Please say what else you required, a thing which you wanted right down here. You should not go to Quetta in night time due to Stormy weather, in my opinion you should go in morning time. here you will not get standard time of Drinking, here you will get low time of Drinking. Yours B— D—.'

Stuart thanked the now beaming innkeeper, handed back the glass and assured him we had all we wanted. At last he went, and we were able to snuggle down into our sleeping-bags, laughing a little, and wondering about that 'Low time of Drinking' — perhaps they distilled some spirit of their own 'right down here', the gin had tasted peculiar enough. We slept peacefully then, still rocked slightly by the dying wind as if we were at sea.

The next morning we left at half-past four, well before daybreak. But it was not earlier than the Afghans; they were already on the road, and they made an unforgettable sight caught dramatically in our headlights as we moved slowly through their trains. Each one of the great sandy, loping camels stood out as if heavily limned with black against the outline of the next ahead; each with its swaying, nodding blanketed figure atop, a cluster of white puppies, a huddle of new-born lambs, or hens with fluttering wings, and even a goat or two — rearing a long black satyr's neck gauntly to the stars, like some dark Dionysian sacrifice There was little noise now — only an endless but slight melodious jangle of camel bells, and sometimes a hoarse voice shouting at the herds. It was a remarkable experience; like a vision carved out of the night.

At some point before daybreak we had left the herds behind, so we paused for a quick toilet, and brewed up water for tea in the volcano kettle. With dawn, the deadly flat landscape changed, and range upon range of rosy, misted, sun-touched mountains stood revealed ahead above vast golden cornfields. As the clouds began to lift still more, so the ethereal colours deepened, and the sun touched the more westerly higher ranges so that they seemed to be floating in a haze of blue shadow.

We were coming up rapidly towards the Bolan Pass. It was a serenely golden day after the storm, the mountains were ever-deepening cerulean and pink against a mild sky of duck-egg blue — tones as soft as a sigh, although the outlines were fiercely wild and barren.

Not so very long ago the sixty-mile march through the Bolan Pass used to take six full days. Now the road is good, winding sometimes beside the river under great cliffs and caves; and everywhere again we passed the Afghans on the move. As we climbed into the hills, still more distant mountains unfolded, in their cobalts and flushed rose as delicate as a screen of silks. Only a few sharp accents relieved this sunfilled, pastel landscape; the dark madder brown of nomad tents, and the rich red of the women's flying skirts and shawls; that stood out against the light stone of river bed and cliff.

Beyond 'Windy Corner' tunnel, a dead camel among the boulders belied the morning serenity of the place, and served a little to emphasize the true character of this long, stony pass to Quetta.

9

Baluchistan and the Persian Desert

We reached Quetta early that afternoon : there we bought a news-paper, our first for several days, and learnt sadly of the death of another friend; the first Paramount Ruler of Malaya. We read the news with sorrow, recalling gay informal family parties at the Astana, formal occasions too, and—most vividly—the last time we had seen His Majesty, when we had been summoned to say goodbye one morning in Kuala Lumpur.

Quetta was a good resting-place, quiet and civilized, a neat little garrison town surrounded by barren snow-flecked mountains. Forty years ago ravaged by earthquake it has a strange white, other-worldly, light about it, and everything—especially the mountains pale in the sunlight against pale cerulean skies—looks as if it were cut out in the flat. But the people of Quetta are very real and human and extremely friendly; our room bearer, a rag-ged but charming man with a heart-warming smile, patiently tried each day to instil into us a little Urdu.

It was a delight to bath frequently again, to eat well, and at night to fall asleep by firelight. We lingered here for a few days; Ark was serviced; and we indulged in a shopping spree—a Baluchi embroidered cap of mirrors for my hat collection, an irresistible cape of snow lynx skins from the mountains, and an embroidered waistcoat for Stuart. We met two parties of Australians travelling overland to England from Bombay : two young men with their scared young wives in a Volkswagen-Kombi like the Ark, and a delightful, stalwart Yorkshire-born couple in a landrover. Because the two girls were so nervous, the landrover pair had agreed to join forces, and travel in convoy. They went on ahead of us, but we were to fall in with them again later.

In the hotel we heard that an Italian couple had recently come through all the way from Europe in only fifteen days. But we did not intend to try record-breaking; allowing for sand-storms, break-

downs and punctures, we expected to be a week or even ten days
on the road to Isfahan.

We put Ark into purdah in preparation for the desert, thinking
it would be like the Jacobabad area; a removable yashmak for the
windscreen, and a small port side curtain to shield the passenger
seat. She had a rather coy, Middle Eastern air in this outfit; the
cloth was gay printed stuff from the local market and toned well
with the other curtains. In the market we also stocked up with
food and fruit, and the salted pistachio nuts and dried apricots
that are a speciality of Quetta; now we were ready and strong to
face the long run of 1,240 miles through Baluchistan and the
Persian Desert.

On April 7th, six days behind our planned date, we left Quetta
early in the morning on one of the ancient migratory routes of
prehistoric times which for centuries have linked East and West. It
was a grey morning of short rain showers; ahead, the road glistened silvery, losing itself around the dark shoulder of a hill. A
mile or so out of Quetta there was a signpost :

> 'London 5,887 miles.
> Kila Safed 392 miles.
> Nushki 83 miles.'

Then it was like Dartmoor in the rain, with a faint rainbow
over the hills and a high wind; the mountains to the right were
threateningly black; the little road stretching away, a narrow
ribbon twisting into the dreaded wilderness of Baluchistan.

Presently the sun came out; at once the distant hills changed to
plum colour and deep blue; some dark tents of nomadic shepherds
lay in a brown hollow of the bleak foothills : an inky sky, shafts
of sunlight, weird changing effects of angry clouds and purple
hills and sunlit sandy foreground. . . .

The few squat mud hut villages were so much a part of the low,
barren landscape that they might have been there since the ice
age.

Around each pass, each bend or each wadi the landscape
opened out ever wider, more vast and more lonely—the endless,
endless hills painted with fitful sun and with cloud shadow. At
the sound of our engine a few terrified, fat-tailed Pakistan sheep
dashed off, madly scrambling over the stones; and despite the
barrenness of the land there were many flocks of little birds that

swooped and dipped before the Ark like dolphins pacing a boat. We passed a village with the appropriate name of Ash-Khan; a tiny round mosque, strange graveyards of spiky shale. . . .

The hills, mere tortured shaley triangles, black-edged and sharp-needled, thrust up into sworls and peaks in wildly contrasting angles of strata. Then we approached a big granite escarpment, and the weird illusions of the sands began.

We were quite alone. Now to the left lay a series of apparently endless rock ridges, a host of black peaks, with ochreous sand-drifts creeping up their eastern facing flanks. To the right, and ahead were vaporous blue, unreal hills; changing shapes, and this mysterious unreality of the wastes. Lava-like screes had poured down the black hills; a haze of a blue dust storm scudded across the distant sand barrier . . . Sand was creeping nearer to the road, blowing across it now in golden gusts. We were driving into a grey-white heat and dust; spiralling dust-devils rose angrily, sweeping across the plain to those barren rock ridges in the west. It was getting hot now, and there was a broiling up of the dust, like flies. We stopped to fix Ark's purdah : ahead the shining coal-black peaks of this long ridge of mountains loomed higher and still higher out of the dust haze, the road going on into nothingness beyond them. . . .

The sands beat like a sea against the coal-black cliffs. In all this wilderness, silent and yet magnificent stood a gnarled, ancient bent casuarina, a dark and ghoulish tree. Here we stopped for a few moments; we were very small and lonely in this strange, wonderful country, that was ravaged by earthquakes, split, torn, wildly rent, starkly awe-inspiring.

For sixty-five miles the road skirted that range of gleaming black hills, and there was no life or movement but the waves of the sand beating against the dark cliffs.

We scarcely saw a living soul; only one or two lonely groups of P.W.D. road workers, who waved and saluted eagerly as if glad to see a car. There were a few ruined buildings and caravanserais, and some stone-marked prayer spots, facing Meccawards. As the grimly black mountains grew higher, a salt plain appeared ahead, white against the pearl-grey sky. It was evident that any rain that fell poured off those slatey cliffs and rushed across the road, for many of the shallow wadis were broken right away.

The road diverged a little now towards the east, towards the salt plain, and then we saw our first mirages : several large lakes about a quarter of a mile ahead, completely illusionary—brilliant blue, with clear reflections of mountains and scrub and sandhills. Each as we drew near, evaporated to the last imaginary drop, only to open out again behind in a sheen of widening blue. A common-place of the desert, I know, but to us the first sight of it was impressive. There were some tiny huts of mud and straw, a police post with an ominous battered notice : 'KNOCK FOR HELP', and then we thought we saw the trees of Dalbandin oasis, like skyscrapers in the distance. But probably it was yet another mirage.

We plugged on for miles; the blue 'lakes' widening, telescoping, vanishing, only to re-emerge and multiply behind. At last we came to the oasis : the skyscrapers dwindled to date palms and a few mud-walled houses in the sand. It actually was Dalbandin; and we turned in past the little Resthouse to buy petrol in the can from a Militia post nearby.

The Resthouse, built by the British during the 1914-18 war, stands around three sides of a square. It is made of wood and stone with a pleasing mat and mud roof set on bamboo poles. In one corner of its garden is a little graveyard, where young British soldiers killed in frontier battles lie buried.

In the last war the British embellished this garden with the addition of a small swimming-pool, now used entirely, it seems, for prayer ablutions and for drinking water. It made a perfect foil and mirror for the rich dark fronds of the date palms and the softer casuarinas all around. The tennis court that the English had also made in the garden was in use by Pakistani Government officials; the Customs officer among them, a handsome young Pathan, came across to introduce himself and to offer help, if we needed any. While they went on playing, we bathed—in icy water —changed and went outside again to walk in the sand, and watch the gorgeous pale golden balloon of the sun sink down like a harvest moon. It reached the dust layer, dipped, and was gone behind the wilderness. Then its great rays shot up from the earth's rim to touch white clouds to gold in the blue above; the voice of the muezzin rang out from a little mosque in the sand close by, and the white moon began to turn luminous above the date palms.

There were some small black goats tethered on the lawn, and three quiet dogs gathered friendly fashion beside us as we sat down near the pool, the exquisite reflections of dark fronds were fading from the azure surface as dusk fell.

The khanasama brought a simple meal of curried mutton and rice. Presently a young man came and made his prayer ablutions in the swimming-pool, rather ostentatiously, I thought—and correctly—for it was all merely an excuse to come and talk, to practise his English. He was a schoolmaster, a 'failed English B.A.'

Once again we were impressed with this overwhelming eagerness to talk English. But tomorrow we would be in Persia, where, so we thought, French and German were more popular tongues. This was the last night in a land that, through the common link of one-time British rule still seemed a bridge to our former life.

We said goodnight to the young schoolmaster, and were just thinking about bed, when headlights flashed at the opening in the mud wall, and the khanasama ran to unlock the gates. It was a landrover : its occupants two exhausted young men, one in a bad state of nerves. A New Zealander driving from England, already two years on the road, and a Dutchman who had joined up with him somewhere. They spoke of the horrors they had come through in Persia, of breakdowns, delays, shifting sands and other ordeals. But somehow we did not feel over-perturbed; we got the impression that they were exhausted, possibly ill-fed, and no doubt lacking sleep. So after talking a little, we left them to their food and withdrew to bed.

We were ready to go at first light. Men were saying their dawn prayers, and making their ritual ablutions under the date palms as we left. The Customs officer had told us that there were twenty miles of fairish road before the bad began. We hoped to reach Zahedan that night, the first town in Persia, 241 miles away— which does not sound much but on such roads is a good distance. Nok-Kundi is the Pakistan Customs station some miles west of Dalbandin, a bleak mud village where I think travellers generally stay, but Dalbandin was infinitely more attractive. After the Pakistani Customs there is a kind of no man's land, a stretch of sixty miles to the actual frontier at Kila Safed.

At Nok-Kundi we asked if the Bombay-London bus had gone through yet and hearing that it had not, we left a letter for our shipboard friends, the Fords.

It was a gravel road now, through a flat waste of black stones;

once again there were the extraordinary visual illusions; a square mud-walled Militia post by the road with a casuarina tree inside looked like an immensely tall building with a huge tank on top. Then there was nothing, not even illusions — nothing but black stones as far as the eye could see all around to the horizon. The wind got up : sand began to fly madly into the van. A line of white stones marked the stone road, and the telegraph line marked the railway. So universally colourless was it, that I got out Fisher's *The Middle East,* and read aloud to Stuart for hours on end until my voice cracked. The road although of gravel, was not like the 'washing board' type that we met later in Persia.

Stones, stones; salt and sands, sands; howling tearing winds, nothing to relieve the desolation but a few hillocks . . . all was nothingness. . . .

We were very grateful to Fisher that day, for the precise and masterly manner in which he described the nature of the lands we were approaching; the extraordinary geography; the horror of the Dasht-i-lut; the poverty of the farmers and herdsmen whose total income is often only £10, and not more than £25 a year. . . .

Then in the middle of nowhere there appeared a man, pushing a bicycle in the centre of the road, the wind being too strong to ride against. He waved warmly, even gaily.

So people did appear in this wilderness after all . . . But he seemed to be the only one . . . Twenty miles still to go of this frontier land — high wind, stones and chips, dust and shale. We began to think we had lost the elusive Kila Safed. In fact it was twenty-three miles beyond where it was supposed to be in this most infernally desolate region. Road and surroundings were still all of this same drab colour, the sky too now was a grey-white dust-filled bowl, and now there was no life at all, not even a bird or a beetle. Strips of salt only enlivend the nightmare scene : never before this had I really known what was meant by a 'howling desolate waste'. Then to the east appeared a wall of hills, layer after layer of Dantesque inferno-like hills, sharp — veiled in hot blown sand.

We reached the Baluchi frontier at three o'clock in the afternoon; it was Kila Safed at last : 'Right-hand drive in Iran'. But the Customs post was still further on, at Mirjawa.

Small barren hills began to step down nearer to the road; they were bright coloured — red, purple, beige and verdigris.

To the south, suddenly there were tents and men in a bleak waste that sloped down to nothingness, a colourless sunbaked vacuum. The men, far away, stood in a long row, like midgets, digging vaguely with picks and spades in this sand-buffeting wind, this screaming grey hell.

Beyond them, to the west there appeared a fort, like a child's sand castle—but it was a ruin. Then suddenly and unaccountably, there were patches of green wheat; unbelievably wheat!

The road deteriorated to a broken mass of salt-caked mud, and we rattled down miserably over grey transverse ruts into a wadi. We had come to Mirjawa.

The Persian douane was in a large square mud-walled caravanserai of a place. It was a holiday, the chief official was away and everyone seemed concerned because I was a writer. They had received a signal about me from somewhere—the official in Delhi, perhaps—we waxed cautious. I sat in the back trying to look weak and innocent, pointing to the 'pin-ups' of the boys, shaking my head over the newspapers for which they guessed I wrote; producing cooking-pots—if, as we thought, it were a sin to write, then I was housewife and mother too. French was of no avail, someone who spoke Italian was called in, but that was of little help. The official kept reiterating: 'Mrs *Katharine* and Mr *Alexander** . . . Mrs* Katharine's car . . .?' After a while, I forget quite how, perhaps we all wearied of the game, we were released and drove on towards Zahedan.

Beyond the frontier there were stark pyramid-shaped hills; and after many, many more miles we saw a couple of small birds, and a hawk; soon there must be some human life. I thought I saw a mud village away in the distance, but Stuart said: 'In this land it may only be a heap of camel dung.' Such are the illusions.

Now, there stood on our left some big, awe-inspiring hills, pale sand stretching to their dark bases. Here we stopped for a few minutes and I walked away a little towards these antique hills. It was silent but for the wind in the camel scrub, and so eerie that one would not have been surprised to see a dinosaur or some such lost prehistoric beast come ponderously out of the gullies and across the bleak stones and sand towards one. Behind me on the road Ark waited; a small, bright little haven of modern civilization, an only too vulnerable anachronism, in which we had pierced

* Stuart's first name.

this lost landscape : I was glad to turn away from those dreadful but marvellous hills, back to the twentieth century again.

I often thought as we went through these wonderful landscapes how many times I had looked down on similar places from the air, as the plane had left Karachi for Bahrein, or Baghdad for Cairo, over Baluchistan or the Sinai, and how much I had longed to see more closely these lonely scalloped hills and ridges and rifted lunar valleys of rust and ochre.

Then, quite suddenly, I saw a tower ahead : a white tower standing up in the desert. But — no, not a tower after all : the tail of an areoplane — on Zahedan airstrip. We had arrived.

In Persia the different racial characteristics of the people were at once obvious; we were now among men who seemed closer to the Mediterranean type than to the Indo-Aryan. After the tall gaunt men of Pakistan, these people looked much more like Latins, shorter, more compact, with oval faces, and dark side whiskers. It seemed a big step out of the Orient that we had taken in those few hundred miles of empty land.

We went to the only hotel in Zahedan, to find it fully occupied by the Australian party of seven, plus two Germans, all delayed a day as it was the Sabbath, and they had to wait for a Bank to open. There was nowhere to park the car at the hotel, but we agreed to dine with them, and went off to the police station, having been told that Persian police stations were good parking places if nothing else were available. We reported our arrival to the blue-coated rather dashing-looking police, who agreed that we might sleep at their gates and more or less under their protection.

We were just starting to wash off the top coatings of sand, making up our beds and Stuart had poured a drink each, when a policeman knocked on the door, popped his head in and asked vaguely : 'Are you Mrs *Katharine*?'

My heart sank, what *had* I done now? Stuart hopped out quickly onto the pavement, and in the excitement I upset my drink on my only clean skirt. I was struggling to change into another when he returned, grinning all over his face. The Governor of Zahedan himself had arrived, in a large American car, and we were invited to dine with him, and to sleep at the Governor-General's new house. I hastily finished dressing, and we were swept away literally out of the gutter, under the obviously flabbergasted eyes of the smart police. It was a Cinderella-like situation which afforded us both a certain amount of satisfaction and amusement.

We didn't forget that we had ordered dinner at the hotel and informed the Governor; it was nothing—no trouble at all, a message of cancellation would immediately be sent. First, we were shown the rooms that we were to use in the Governor-General's newly-built unoccupied house: separate rooms with single beds; all this time I think the Persian officials had been uncertain of our married status. We explained that we would like to be in one room, and the Governor at once arranged for the beds to be moved. We then went to his own house to talk—over sweetmeats, marrow seeds, salted nuts, pistachios and apricot kernels, and little glasses of clear tea. His wife was away in Teheran, and he apologized that dinner would not be as it should had she been home. But we enjoyed it, our first Persian meal: the rice was lemon-flavoured and with it were served kebabs, delicious curds, sprigs of fresh mint, spring onions and aubergine chutney, and to drink there was araka, the Persian vodka.

The drawing-room was thickly laid with modern Persian carpets, one was a large red Kerman, a type that does not particularly appeal to me personally, but in a deep window recess was a beautiful prayer mat, a bride's mat of silk. An antique with a charming repeat design, I should think it was a museum piece and of great value.

After dinner we were escorted back to the Governor-General's house, and left in the charge of its only occupant, an armed guard who slept in a room near the door equipped with an immense silver samovar. The floor of our room had deep layers of Persian carpets set one upon the other lavishly, on the beds were large quilts to which the sheets were sewn. The window was blocked up with animal wool and with newspapers, but we managed to open it a crack against the sand piled up on the window ledge. All this gave one an inkling of what winter must be like here, almost in Central Asia. Along the passage, in the very core of the building were two lavatories, with no water except that which stood in the usual exquisitely-shaped *kalasa* style bronze water jar, and no drainage except into the foundations.

This method, the same as that of the Nepalese, seemed here all the more remarkable in the heart of a brand-new mansion, built for a Governor-General; how it is managed and endured is hard to understand. Do people move when the smell becomes too unbearable, or does the question somehow solve itself? One might well think that in time the house would begin to walk.

There were no baths, but there were two modern wash-basins in the same central lobby; we made a very hasty toilet, and galloped back to bed. In the morning we awoke far too early, it was broad daylight at half-past five — we had forgotten to alter our watches, we must have gone to bed at eight-thirty by Pakistan time, ten-fifteen by Persian time. We washed and dressed, and began hoping for tea, not quite liking to boil up the volcano kettle in the new garden lest we should appear too independent. We eventually met the large and cheerful guard who willingly brewed some of Basant's tea on his tall samovar. Presently the Governor's cook arrived with hot eggs in a napkin, and a plate of hot unleavened bread, our first taste of the *nams** of the Middle East, a dish of thick golden honey to eat with them, and more tea.

The samovar was another reminder that we were on the brink of Europe as well as of Central Asia: the true East was now behind us, this was thirty degrees north — a marked transition. No wonder those four hundred bleak miles of Baluchistan form a barrier. Baluchistan and Afghanistan are walls dividing the west from the east, walls cut by those grim, migratory highways of antiquity; for it is still really only a relatively wealthy few who straddle those barriers by air, and need to think nothing of the change. Only the road conveys any inkling of what it must mean to the masses; to the herdsmen, the nomads, and the static populations.

As we still had to wait some little time until the Bank opened, one of the smart policeman helped us buy Persian Vodka, Gulf of Oman tuna from Bender Abbas, and white wine from Shiraz. At the Bank we met the Australians, they were also moving on that day; on the whole they travelled much faster than we did as we stopped more frequently to paint or photograph, and were rather inclined to nurse the Ark over the 'washing board' surface. Some drivers prefer to take the ridges at forty or fifty miles an hour in order to skim over the tops; it does not work out too badly that

---

* *Nams* are oven-baked on hot stones, and occasionally the stones come with the bread, so one has to be careful of one's teeth.

The Shah's Bridge at Isfahan

Persian carpets for sale deep in the *souks* of Isfahan

The six remaining gigantic columns of the Temple of Jupiter at
Ba'albek, Lebanon

way with a landrover, but a vehicle like the Volkswagen gets into a dreadful bounce, and it feels as I imagine it would to ride a bucking steer. Even driving as we did, at the end of the day one usually had a muscular tension in the thigh as if one had been riding a horse. Having got used to the Indian wallop it was now necessary to learn a new way of sitting tight on the Persian bounce, and I shot under the dashboard once or twice before I acquired the art.

When we were ready to leave Zahedan, we went to say goodbye to the Governor in his office; tea of course was immediately served, the Persian custom; little glasses of clear tea in silver holders.

At the foot of the Afghan Pass we caught up again with the Australian contingent, who were lunching. But after a brief pause to speak with them, we pushed on into the pass itself. It was a most attractive lunching spot : small islands of weather-beaten casuarinas growing in the sand in the very heart of the pass gave shelter from the burning sun. It was beautiful, the hills streaked with colour, blackberry, purple, jade and tan, and we lingered on in the shade of the casuarinas, eating *nams* and tuna, drinking white wine, and painting. The Australians soon passed by, the two young men with their nervous wives, and the cheerful bronzed couple in the landrover.

The Afghan Pass was not at all as we had expected, after hearing alarming tales of it; and on that sunny spring day it tempted one to linger, but the afternoon was going, and the shifting sands of Bam still lay ahead. At last we pushed on too, and came swiftly down into the great salt plain on the edge of the ghastly Dasht-i-Lut, bound on the south by the Zagros Mountains, and on the north by the Elburz, the rivers draining wastefully into the central salt pans.

Between Zahedan and Kerman the map ominously marks 'loose sands'; the Bam area which we had dreaded most. But it was beautiful as we came down towards it; the sand dunes were enormous, the famous 'walking dunes', and I could not resist scrambling to the top of one. The view was magnificent : the Zagros Mountains dark to the south; the Afghan Pass behind and, standing away to the north stretching down towards the terrible salt wastes, were serried ranks of dunes, each one blown to a sharp-cut crescent-shaped top. On that sunny afternoon they looked harmless, but this was the place where only a year or two previously some travellers like ourselves had been lost. Overnight, the

G

dunes had moved across the road blotting it out, and in attempting
to find a way around to the north the travellers became hopelessly
stuck. The dunes shifted back again cutting them off, the traffic
continued as usual along the road, and it was not until weeks later
that by some chance they were found—dead in their vehicle.

I recalled this now with a shiver of fear. I knew that I must not
delay. On the track below Ark looked extremely small and lonely,
Stuart waved to me to come down and I ran back to him quickly :
a storm could get up at any time.

Every few miles, in this wilderness a gang of four or five P.W.D.
road workers would make beseeching kissing gestures, indicating
that they wanted cigarettes, and we flung out as many as we
reasonably could. The mirage illusions returned : men looked like
trees; a truck in its dust cloud like a locomotive; a ruined caravanserai half buried in the sand was surely a mountain.

Then later, while I was driving, we saw the tower of which we
had read. It was no illusion, it was a real tower built of brick,
standing in the middle of emptiness, presumably as a landmark
for travellers in this area of shifting sands. Without it, we certainly would not have known which track to take, and could easily
have been lost here.

It was late, we had fallen silent now, we wanted to get through
to Bam if possible before dark. But only just beyond those unpleasant loose sands we passed a rather dilapidated Opal saloon,
I slowed down and stopped. A young fair man with a girlish face
came to the driving cab; he spoke German and his manner was
oddly restrained, he did not look much more than seventeen.
There was a girl with him, perhaps a year older than he. She had
long, blonde dyed hair; she wore cotton slacks, and a loose knitted
jumper of pale mauve wool and clearly nothing on at all under
it, and she was a big-breasted girl. In contrast to the boy she
seemed absolutely calm, even gay. With our few words of German
we understood that they were returning from India. They had a
a puncture, and could we give them some water? Certainly we
could; we carried gallons. They must have been extremely thirsty
for they drank like parched creatures. Stuart helped to mend the
puncture; they had no patches, and practically no tools. 'Mauve
jumper's' eyebrow tweezers came in handy; she travelled with her
cosmetics in a little tin box.

No sooner had Stuart helped to patch them up, than they shot away abruptly into the desert in a cloud of dust, as if they were taking off in a road race. Ark trundled on gently in their wake, Stuart driving now. The sun was getting low, the wind howling off the sands, and we would be glad to reach Bam. But we had gone only a few miles when we came upon the Germans again : another tyre now was flat in the sand. Again we got out, and while Stuart and the boy tinkered with glue and patches, I took a closer look at their car, for I was becoming mystified. How could people be mad enough to travel in this desert with no water, and no tools ? Who could they be ? On the back seat were two Army sweaters, two grimy towels, nothing else. Also the 'D' for Deutschland was not a metal plate; it had merely been pencilled on a paper disc and carefully stuck on; a good imitation. In the boot, which the boy opened in search of a tool there was only a badly-slashed spare wheel, and a small zipper bag, open and bursting with soiled linen. My curiosity was really aroused, sane people simply do not travel through the wastes of Baluchistan and Persia in such a state and in such a car without some peculiar and urgent reason.

It seemed as if the patch would not stick; half an hour or more passed, and then the boy said that he would wait until a truck came and gave him air for the other tyre. It was almost dark but there was nothing more that we could do. I gave them slabs of chocolate, several oranges, and more water, though incredibly they had only one empty Coco-cola bottle each for me to fill.

Feeling a little guilty we left them there by the roadside : Bam was about fifteen miles ahead, and we would report their presence.

It was quite dark now; the circular humps of qanats, and the squat houses of a small mud village or two loomed close to the road, the surface was shocking. We paused only briefly to eat a little food in the dark, and then drove on to Bam. We were extremely puzzled by the German couple, wondering how they had come to travel in such a way. It looked absurdly as if they were week-ending in the East; as if one night in Berlin, they had said to each other—'Let's go to India !' and had gone, just as they were, without one thought more.

Unfortunately they remain a query, although the Australians who also encountered them several times, did later make some suppositions about the pair, and added a little to the story. Some Persian mystic said :

'If thou art a wanderer
From door to door,
Close thine eyes
To the fault of others.'

It was not the faults of this pair that intrigued me, but the mystery.

Bam was a very small Persian town huddled in the dark. Had we had more experience we would have slept in the desert that night, but I am glad we did not, for we should have missed an attractive courtyard, the Bam police station. It was a mosque-like building, foursquare around a central pool, extremely difficult to reach. In the almost pitch dark night somebody led us down a long narrow passage, so angled that it was only possible to enter the courtyard under an archway by making an elaborate turning.

The long central pool was overhung by a splendid green vine heavy now with half-ripe grapes. At one side, under a recessed arch and walls patterned with designs in blue and gold quotations from the Koran, was a kind of raised platform on which we were invited to sleep. A pomegranate tree was in full flower at one end of the courtyard, and around the pool were little heart-shaped beds of pansies set among the flagstones. There was just room for Ark between the surrounding terrace and the flower-beds, and we were soon in our sleeping bags, sardine fashion on our comfortable bed. I fell asleep thinking of old Omar Khayyam, for this lovely courtyard was Persia, as I'd imagined it, with the vines and the pomegranates.

In the morning a young boy arrived to take down details from our passports. Throughout Persia the police summon schoolboys to assist in dealing with travellers' papers, a point that surprised and rather pleased us. These children, of the fourteen to sixteen-year-old-group, had been learning English for two or three years, and later when they had satisfied the police, they invariably wanted to talk — to show us their exercise books, learn the names and ages of our own children, their standard of education and so forth. To us this was one of the most remarkable and cheering things that occurred on the trek. We had felt our own lingual deficiences for we spoke virtually only English and Malay; we had expected to hear German and French in Persia, but it was not so, the coming generation is learning English, and with an English accent. The further one went into the Middle East the more impressive was this fact.

That day we passed through little walled Persian villages, where clear open streams ran beside the road under the poplars. In the village fields men were busy tilling the earth with spades, and sometimes they worked in quartets with beautiful synchronized rhythm like dancers. We lunched in a long bleak pass on the road to Kerman, and some shy smiling shepherds came for cigarettes. This was the country of qanats, some of which were being repaired. It is a wonderful system of carrying water, an absolute network of these underground channels still webs the countryside, but when the hordes of Ghengis Khan sacked Persia in the third decade of the thirteenth century these marvellous irrigation works which had been maintained for centuries, fell into disrepair.

Kerman was full of stinging dust, cold and windswept. This city of famous carpets did not appeal to us. It is notorious also for an appalling act of cruelty when, after an eighteenth century siege, the eunuch king and founder of the Qajar dynasty had the eyes of 11,000 people plucked out and, so it is said, counted every eye himself to make quite sure all were there.

We should have done better to have slept outside in the desert, but the wind was so appalling that we thought to find a little shelter in the town. There was nowhere to stay, that we could reach in Ark, so again we took refuge with the police, but were not allowed to park inside their compound, and had to resort to the gutter once more. One young policeman, Isfahani-born, told us to take heart. 'Isfahan', he said, '—is not like Kerman, the wind doesn't blow there as it does all day here. Isfahan is—is—the *world*.'

At the time I thought he was trying to say the best place in the world, but I realized later that he was searching for a translation of the Persian saying: 'Isfahan *is* half the world.'

We passed a dull but sheltered night in the gutter, and pushed on very early in the morning. A few miles out of the town we had carburettor trouble, and to our shame found that sand was thick in the oil-air filter; we were busy scraping this out with a spoon when the Australian landrover passed, going back to Kerman with the older Australian and one of the young men. They stopped, and said that the others were in trouble, they had run out of water, had some bother with the fan and were now laid up with two punctures only a mile ahead. The wind had dropped during the afternoon and they had all camped just west of the town. We went on to join them, and the other young man helped Stuart with the carburettor.

The three women were sitting in the van, looking cold and rather dejected, and because the high wind had again got up they were unable to brew a hot drink. The wind was icy, but I soon got warm running about collecting sage brush fuel for the volcano kettle, it was always a godsend for the higher the wind the better it burns. The women said afterwards that they thought I had gone quite crazy rushing about the desert apparently gathering invisible flowers, but they changed their minds when I brought them some hot tea, and soon they were all out too helping me collect scrub for several more brews while we waited for the landrover to return.

We lost five hours in time that day, but we made some good friends. The Wrights, the Yorkshire-born couple in the landrover, decided to go on that morning leaving the others to wait while their fan was repaired; and we agreed to camp with them later at about five o'clock when we should be able to catch up.

That evening we saw the landrover drawn off the road, just about where we had arranged to camp, on the plateau short of Anar. It was 5,000 feet above sea level here, and intensely cold at night, but it was a wonderful evening; the sun set dramatically behind two volcano-like hills, as the full moon was rising. We placed the two vehicles so that our camp formed an L-shape, affording some protection from the wind. After supper we invited the Wrights to coffee and Quetta brandy, and it was snug talking in Ark with the oil lamp burning on the table.

The next morning we got up at five o'clock; Stuart boiled the volcano kettle in a howling wind and made tea for the four of us.

The moon was still brilliant in the west, although the east was already light. We agreed to camp again with the Wrights at about the same time in the evening. As we left camp the sun came up like a sudden shout in the east; at once the snow mountains were flushed with pink, and the two volcano-shaped hills turned to a soft rose-red; then, at the same instant, the moon set huge and pale behind them.

A magnificent start to the day. Although it was cold early the sun was soon warming, it was a divine blue and gold morning and we were increasingly happy and elated, pleased to be a little more at home in the desert, and grateful to the Wrights for having helped us to be so. Now that we had slept in the desert its seduction set in rapidly. Its beauty haunts me, and always will until I can get out into it again, its peace is comparable only to that of the underwater coral world which I also love, but in so different a way, and yet both have something akin — clarity of lighting, and the washed brilliance of colours.

There were 1,500 miles, or so we reckoned, of Persian bounce between Zahedan and Teheran,* but the days spent on them were remarkably happy ones. We began to acquire the nomad's ways with economy of water; washing our lunch spoons and forks in our evening soup, and dry-cleaning our plates with tissues. It was a wonderful life, one decent wash-up a day sufficed. Besides water, fuel too was becoming a problem, and we would stop for any really worthwhile chips dropped by lorries. This was our fourth bathless day, but we did not feel unduly dirty : one washed at night, sometimes I confess partly in the washing-up water, and then rinsed out one's smalls in the tooth water. I don't know if the dryness of the air acts as an antiseptic, but dirt seems to be almost a thing of the past.

The Wrights overtook us during the morning. We encountered some nasty wadis that day, and at one we met a Persian who asked for a lift, his car was stuck with a broken axle. He was a big, heavy man, and with his extra weight I doubt if we should have got through the next steep wadi if there had not happened to be in it a gang of road-workers. He yelled to them to push like mad and we just made it against the fast-running stream.

Beyond this wadi, the Wrights were very considerately waiting for us, to ensure Ark had come through unscathed.

We dropped our large Persian at the next village, where he could get help, and went on.

Yedz was a pleasant little town, its shops full of crystal sugar, carpets and vodka, and the biggest *nams* I had yet seen. There were rice fields around the town; some interesting bottle-glass domed-roof houses like flying saucers which I think were public baths, and many summer cellars, with tall wind towers, for it is so hot here in the summer months that people retreat underground.

Then we were out on the road towards Nain, and the surface was such that the wheel frequently went crazy under one's hands,

* Some people call this 'the longest cart track in the world.'

but the serrated peaks of the Zagros were as sharp in profile as horns and the mountains to the west a fabulously pearly pink, as delicate as spun gold thread, and blue too with the brilliant light of sapphires.

That night the other Volkswagen caught up, and with it and the landrover we camped, short of a little place called Bambiz Pa'in. It was a sociable evening, like the last night of a voyage, the last out from Isfahan, and although the two girls insisted on spending it in washing their clothes which they hung in the moonlight on a line between their van and ours, the two young men, the Wrights and ourselves gathered in Ark over coffee and vodka, and someone brought a bottle of red wine. There was a lovely fug and plenty of animated talk around the oil lamp. The white cold light of the moon on the desert outside, and the thought of the blue mosques of Isfahan ahead were stimulating.

Before Nain, which we reached the next morning, small sand-coloured hills foamed up like fossilized waves. In the little town, famous for its tenth century mosque we stopped to ask the way of some schoolboys. They mobbed Ark eagerly. 'Where are you going?' — 'Have you had breakfast?' — 'Do you know the way to Isfahan?'

Then the road veered south-west to mount up over a 7,000 foot pass. On this our fifth bathless day we were looking forward to a good bath; our hair, now inclined to stand straight up on end, was stiff with dust. On the pass it was intensely cold; there was a sudden hailstorm, at once the hills were white with hail and snow. We had seen our fourth spring and were now back to winter, snow lay on the ground and lined with white the little round roofs of a tiny village. But only just over the crest of the pass there was blossom in a fruit orchard—pink and white blossom in walled orchards, and the silvery green of poplars about to burst into leaf.

Suddenly—as blue as the sea, the plain of Isfahan lay below, the road crossing over it towards a miraged gateway in the hills beyond.

⧉ 10 ⧉

Easter in Isfahan

In the town the apricot blossom was coming out; there were pansies and stocks in the gardens, lilacs were in bloom, the strange silvery oriental planes, the slim poplars and willows were in new leaf, and yet the rough, wild beauty of the desert that lay so close at hand was unforgettable.

We had travelled 1,240 miles from Quetta, and we were muscularly tired after the violent corrugations of the track, but we were both excited too, for there is something about this high desert land, and this incomparable Persian spring which is intensely exhilarating. We had found a modest little hotel, the Siroos, which had two private showers with lavatory and hot and cold across-the-courtyard and we now held the key to one of these as if it were worth its weight in gold, now we could bath and wash our hair again as often as we wished. Some of our friends enjoyed it too, for baths are not easily come by in Isfahan.

It was just before Easter when we arrived on April 13th, and I thought of the homesick young Isfahani* who, in the dust storms of Kerman had tried to tell me that Isfahan was 'half the world'. In this spring it certainly was magical; the fabulous blue bubbles of the domes glistened and gleamed as if polished against blue Persian skies.

I shall not forget my first breathless impression of Isfahan as we drove in from the desert. As usual, someone on a cycle guided Ark, and as we swept through the Maidan the mosques seemed hardly real, their porcelain domes—blue, azure, aquamarine—floated like vast jewels tantalizing, airy, and wonderful. All too swiftly we raced after our cyclist, out of the Maidan into the Chaharbargh and past the gorgeous dome and minarets of the Madresah.

Our hotel was in the Avenue Abbas Abad just off the Chahar-

* Pronounced like an American endearment—'Isfah-hahney'.

bargh. The Chaharbargh is an avenue of great beauty said to have
inspired the Champs Elysées, it is planted with eight rows of trees.
Every evening we walked there, looking at the miniature and
china shops and wandering in the courtyard of the Madresah, the
early eighteenth century theological college and mosque, last of
the Safavid buildings.

In fact we walked over a great deal of Isfahan, and such was its
beauty that we stayed a full eight days—our longest stay anywhere
—and reluctantly gave up the idea of seeing Persepolis and Shiraz.

I found a hot, sheltered spot in the Ali Qapu palace from which
I could see the minarets and the dome of the Musjid-i-Shah rising
above pale ochre-coloured walls—the false fluted backs and
curved roofs of the Maidan—like a vast jewel lucent above wind-
rippled sands. Beyond the mosque a band of green poplars down
by the river held back shapes of dark umbers, sienna and sharp
ultramarine—the hills of the desert that lay so close at hand.

As I sat there perched high above the Maidan, the hot sun burning my bare legs, my head in the shade of the Ali Qapu wall, the
sounds of Isfahan came up sharp and clear. There was the ham-
mering of coppersmiths below, and the voices of school-children
from the schools behind the palace where boys sat cross-legged
doing their lessons out in the hot spring sunshine. But Isfahan is
not a noisy town, there is no wild hooting of horns, and the people
themselves are quiet, and darkly dressed; the women in black or
deep blue *chadar,* an all-enveloping dust-sheet garment, the men
in dark suits; the theologians in thick brown woollen aba and
white turban; the peasants in drab tunics over full black trousers,
little Persian felt skull caps on their heads.

The Maidan, the heart of Isfahan, is almost a third of a mile in
length, bigger than the Place de la Concorde. In the days of Shah
Abbas, it was in this beautiful rectangle that polo was first played,
now nothing remains of the polo-ground but phallic-looking stone
goal-posts eight feet tall. Instead, a water garden, lawns and fountains fill the centre—unfortunately, railed in. The Maidan is alive
with genuine bazaar crafts carried on in the small shops and houses
that line it, and in the parallel lanes behind it. There are copper
and bronze workers, wheelwrights, the makers of bells, of carpets,
of rugs, and of blue-green pottery with patterns of fish swimming
under a rough but pleasing glaze—almost as rich in colour as the
magical domes themselves.

We spent many hours in the Ali Qapu, the seven-storeyed 'Magnificent Gate', it has an airy pavilion-like elegance, the tall slender pillars of its main balcony which served as a grandstand are straight, slim trees. They support a lovely shallow roof of up-springing edges, a superb contrast to the creamy bubble of the Lutfullah dome immediately opposite — which is of a colour as hard to paint as it is to describe. Its delicacy is like that of an opal, and yet there is nothing of the haziness of opals about it. At sunset it glows like burnt cream, laced with viridian and deep blue.

The Ali Qapu is a maze of little frescoed rooms that were used by the Shah for feasting, music and, no doubt, for love-making too. Here he entertained his foreign guests, and from the balcony where a fountain played, he reviewed his troops and watched the polo.

In the Musjid-i-Shah I tried to discover how the incredible brilliance — the blue jewelled effect of Isfahan's ceramics had been achieved. Even as one watches, the colours — more beautiful than any I have ever seen — change against the sky; a dazzling sheen moves with the sun; the domes seem green against cobalt, sea-blue in the shadow, dark sapphire in the belt of Kufic script; then suddenly, turquoise and lighter than the deep hot sky, with an almost metallic touch of emerald at the crest — and lustrous too on the under swelling, breast-like curves that warmly reflect sunny ochre lights striking up from below. The three gold balls on the top are a shining nipple, bright perhaps against a sudden hail storm over the desert beyond.

The effect of this amazing brilliance is achieved by the use of seven colours, plus white : the '*haftrang*' : three blues — cerulean, azure and sapphire; two greens — viridian and a warmer yellowish one; one yellow — a rich chrome; and black very sparingly used. Everywhere the senses are disturbed by beauty — the sweep of the elongated white Kufic script on dark belts of ultramarine; the detail of honeycomb archways; a large still pool of reflections in an echoing courtyard; marble and jasper fonts to hold sherbet for thirsty worshippers; a little tree bursting into fragile spring leaf against a sun-drenched wall. . . .

We wandered dazzled and amazed, drunk on this great 'draught of the blue' for hours, even days, and when we were satiated we would turn for contrast, even respite, to plunge into the clangorous darkness, the chilly dimness of the Royal Bazaar.

I do not know why the *souks* of the Damascus are praised above all in the Middle East, for to my mind the *souks* of Isfahan are incomparably more wonderful. They are a maze of beautifully vaulted lanes and bye-ways, cold, echoing, alive with voices, the sound of hammers and of horse hooves, and the cry of a muezzin's call to prayer. Wandering as we often did, deep in these alleys, where shafts of light slanting down from sun holes in the domed roofs were caught in dust beams and glinted on copper and silver-ware, we saw at noon one day a man spring up from among his fellow copper-smiths seated at their work and chant the mid-day call to prayer. His clear alto, a spine-thrilling, commandingly beautiful resonant voice, rang out over the ceaseless clunking and clanging of the smiths, and echoed down long cold avenues into the heart of Isfahan. No one seemed to take any notice of him. Possibly he was merely practising, or perhaps he enjoyed the sound of his own splendid voice, it was certainly beautiful and sweet.

One morning we walked down the street of the shoe-makers, and found ourselves in the street of the carpet-sellers and of the dyers of cotton and wool. The dark interiors of the dyers' kitchens would have delighted Rembrandt with their chiaroscuro effect — uprising steam; pools of sunlight and narrow shafting beams strik-ing aslant black shadow; through which light and dark moved the figures of men bending over steaming vats, hoisting out armfuls of wool — blue, brown, orange, red, maroon, rose-pink — working all the time as if with feverish energy.

Side by side with the dyers in this labyrinth were small, deep-set torture chambers, where blindfolded camels ceaselessly turned enormous grindstones on ancient creaking wooden wheels to pound vegetable and rock dyes. This was a sight I shall never forget, horrible and yet intrinsically beautiful. Against shafts of dusty light the tall animal half-filled the room; its mouth blood-stained from the diet of thistles it chewed; there was a strong animal smell, and the interminable squeaking of antiquated mechanism. Beyond the camel rooms were mercifully a few machine-powered engines pounding the red from millions of big chillies.

We wandered on through sunlit yards and dark alleys and saw carpets spread for carts to rattle over, for donkeys to urinate upon, hens to pick and scratch. I was horrified; we had our own small, treasured collection — a few Sarouks, one little Isfahan, some camel bag black Bokharas, some prayer mats—and to see carpets treated like this shocked me. But I gathered that it was part of the process of ageing modern 'antiques', to which one should turn a blind eye —we had wandered very deep into the *souks* that day.

After two nights' rest the Australians left; we missed them, particularly the Wrights, for we had got into the habit of joining them once or twice a day at the bar of the Irantour, to warm up and to compare notes. At lunch time on the day they left we walked out into the street to return to our own little hotel, and saw three enormous buses, filthy, plastered in mud and sand—the 'Indiaman', the Bombay-London buses, exactly as Stuart had foreseen. We dashed up, wrenched open the door of the nearest, and there was Roma Ford beaming at us, travel-stained but as cheerful as ever—they had only just arrived and were waiting for hotel arrangements. They introduced us to 'Paddy' Fisher, the leader and owner of the 'Indiaman', and his two drivers—a tall young Englishman and a cheerful Persian, who went by the name of Albert—a good man to have on a trip such as theirs—not only was he physically extremely strong, but he spoke several useful languages—Syrian, Armenian, Russian, Turkish and English.

How lovely it was in Isfahan at dusk as the lights came out in the Madresah minarets! And how peaceful it was to lie in bed in the morning, eating hot *nams* and melon jam while plucking up courage for the dash across the sunlit courtyard to the shower!

I was reading Ansari, the eleventh century Persian mystic.

'. . . be a man
With a heart full of compassion.
Engage not in vain doing,
Make not thy home in the street of lust and desire.
If thou wouldst become a pilgrim on the path
Of love,
The first condition is
That thou become as humble as dust
And ashes.
Remove A from murad (desire), and it becomes murd (man),
He who renounceth desire becometh a man.'

I thought of the Sikh custodian at the Golden Temple, when Stuart wrote the single word 'man'; I glanced across at Stuart, sipping his clear tea, and reading, as he sat half-naked in the sunshine by the wide open window. His beard was growing well now, it suited him splendidly, he looked very fit and slim. I thought that perhaps if we found nothing else on this journey we shall have refound each other; the desert had made us happier perhaps than we had ever been, in a new interdependent way.

I much enjoyed those sunny early mornings in our red ground floor bedroom unlovely as it was; sometimes a shy Persian cat came to visit us, and we would read until the sun came warm through the slim budding planes, those extraordinary silvery grey trees of Persia.

Everywhere in Isfahan the cynical sayings of our old friend Omar Khayyam seemed to come alive, old frescoes and new re-called him with his cup of wine, his books and his beloved singing in the wilderness, even the execrable modern décor which we saw daily in the bar of the Irantour, as we drank our cup of vodka with our friends. Like us, the crews and passengers of the 'India-man' lingered on for a few days in Isfahan, they had taken a buffeting in the desert and were glad of the respite. Paddy Fisher was planing a brief and new diversion to the Caspian, an idea which interested us immensely, for we had long hoped to be able to do the same but had been doubtful; however, they were en-couraging.

When they had gone we sat in the sun on the terrace, while the plump head chambermaid hung up sheets and newly-washed gar-ments to dry on either side of us. I liked that woman, vigorous and always smiling, and she had an endearingly unconventional habit of doing the ironing on the floor, crawling about on the Persian carpets between the manager's desk and his bed—both of which were conveniently placed in the front office which gave onto the beautiful Chaharbagh. The Siroos was undoubtedly a hotel of character.

With red wine or vodka we drank 'snow ice', the only natural water that one can take with impunity in Isfahan, and of course there was always bottled soda water and many glasses of clear tea. One gets rather tired of cleaning one's teeth in soda water or tea, or even in vodka—but that is one of the few minor drawbacks of Isfahan.

We began to get ready to leave—it was going to be a long drive down to Beirut; we replenished our food stocks with slabs of dried fish from the Caspian, real bread, cheese, eggs, butter, oranges, gherkins, dried plums and apricots, and of course vodka. Unfortunately the grey Persian cat, now a regular visitor, ate some of the cheese in the night, but we were well enough equipped and could spare it to her.

On our last morning we went across the river, the Zayandehdrud, to Jolfa, the Armenian 'suburb' of Isfahan.

A local guide book asserted that if you go along beside the river at sunset you will hear 'enchanted lovers singing in the woods'; the woods proved to be delicate groves of saplings, and alas we did not hear the lovers! We several times went down to the bridge built here by Shah Abbas II across the Zayandehdrud, which loses itself as nearly all Persian rivers do in the central salt wastes. The famous bridge was a pleasance with rest rooms for weary travellers, a space for wedding parties, and even rooms where dancers and singers could entertain travellers from the desert.

St Saviours, the Armenian cathedral at Jolfa was built in 1606. There are several churches in Jolfa and at first we lost our way, but were presently guided by a friendly Armenian gentleman, who had been educated in London, and had lived for many years in India. As we walked with him he pointed to the south towards the blue hill we had so often seen from the Ali Qapu behind the great Mosque. 'Towards the mountain', he said, 'there is a great Armenian cemetery.' I told him that I had not seen this on the tourist map, nor read of it in the guide book. He sighed and shook his head.

'Well, no. You see, we are Christians, and these people are all *Muslims. . . .*' As if that explained everything.

Despite his many cruelities Shah Abbas I had permitted Christions to worship in Isfahan—on the condition that they never rang any bells, for bells are something of a provocation to Muslim ears.

It was grim and cold in the cathedral, with its painful frescoes of martyrdom, but outside in the sunshine, the little settlement of Jolfa had a peaceful atmosphere that spring morning—irises were in lavish bloom, and spring flowers abounded.

We thanked our Armenian friend, and returned across the river to the Muslims, the wine, the arak and Omar.

That night, our last in Isfahan, we had intended to go to bed early, but we had callers and stayed up late in consequence. First there was a young man on his way from England to Malaya, who was full of lurid tales of our way ahead, and then we ran into three charming young Danes, medical students who had parked their Volkswagen outside the Siroos' gate. They too had an alarming story to tell — of Teheran, our destination the following day : their van had been stolen, and they had been delayed for two and a half months retrieving it, literally in bits and pieces, until the Shah himself had intervened. But they seemed remarkably philosophical about it all.

We set off the next morning, considerably later than we had intended to, and feeling not a little wary of Teheran.

The Caspian and Mount Ararat

On the way out of Isfahan there were no signposts in English, but there was a large notice-board that said : 'SEE YOU AGAIN'—we hoped it might be so. We hated leaving Isfahan, and we were not particularly looking forward to Qum the Holy City, or now, to Teheran. In Qum recently three Malayans and an Englishman had accidentally knocked a man off his bicycle, which is not really the sort of thing to do in a Holy City, and subsequently in Teheran they had been run into *by* a General—an accident that had resulted in summary imprisonment. This was another of the rather alarming tales we had just been told.

But Ark was performing very strangely and this worried us far more than the travellers' tales. She was, in fact, running so badly that it was not long before we realized it would be quite impossible to reach Teheran that night. She was barely crawling up even slight gradients, and we realized we would have to sleep in the desert, and alone for the first time.

We felt a little depressed but not for long. It was a day of rapidly moving cumulus cloud; soft, white and grey in the deep cobalt blue sky. To the east there were snow peaks of over 11,000 feet—the foothills of the range between us and Kashan—ochre, umber and indigo blue chased over with pale sunshine and cool cloud shadow.

Suddenly the road appeared to be shooting up like a diving board into the sharp brown peaks beyond, under a magnificent cloud ceiling perspective. We gritted our teeth and sat in silence as poor Ark toiled up in bottom gear. But the deepening and intense blue of the distant hills like an echo of the mosques of Isfahan, the sharply-rising dark peaks, streaked with warm burnt-Sienna and Venetian-red made wonderful contrast with the far-off snows. Here and there a herd of mountain sheep stood sharply defined like drops of jet against pale umber slopes and foothills of

H

a strange acid green. The scenery grew more and more colourful and impressive heralding the Elburz Mountains to the north. Long rocks of red and greenish grey now protruded from the upper layers of red and ochre, like the half-buried bodies of giants, with only thighs and buttocks revealed as if struggling in a vast land-slide.

This giant's bottom type of hill was a geological effect that we were to see constantly from now on throughout the Middle East in varying degrees. The smaller of these rounded ridges gave me the impression that they might have inspired the original mud and brick dome Persian house.

At eighteen miles from Qum we camped, just before sunset. We need not have worried; it was a splendid place in a little dry wadi on the side of a dark hill that sloped down to the west, and the herds were just going home. This was a lesson we soon learnt—to camp between the herds as they went home and so avoid calling attention to our presence. Above the dark shoulder of the hill some easterly snow peaks showed, pink in the sunset glow. Below our open, westward-facing doors the brown slopes fell away to a trickle of a river and rose again darkly to the blue of hills against a sunset sky of gold. Stuart, his hair blowing madly in the wind, tried out the transistor set, sophisticated music sounded strange in these bare archaic hills.

No one disturbed us; only a solitary lorry driver slowed down, and called out to offer help. We had already came to like these Persian lorry drivers immensely, they are among the best and most considerate drivers in the world. Their trucks are huge; taller than a London bus and considerably wider, often as many as four men sit in the driver's cab, above which is a kind of ornamented balcony frequently crowded with a little herd of sheep or goats, riding on high, and peering out with interest like people in a grandstand. Alongside any of these trucks, Ark seemed dwarfed, the driver towered above our heads. We missed these men later on, especially in Syria and in the Lebanon where the standard of driving is appalling.

We left our first lone camp at half-past five the next morning, there was a lark singing in the desert, and we saw several beautiful birds, like tropical sunbirds with viridian green bellies—and also some skittish little hoopoes, dapper and enchanting creatures.

We passed through Qum and crawled on to Teheran, and were

presently rewarded with a splendid view of the great 18,000 foot
peak of Damavand towering up above multicoloured layers of
flat-topped hills that mark the approach to the Elburz range, with
its wall of snows rising so abruptly behind Teheran. This was
civilization again, and we met a number of cars on the road bearing Sabbath pilgrims to the Holy City of Qum.

I do not know how it is that one always seems to arrive at
Muslim towns on a Friday—the Sabbath. Today was Friday, so
once again a garage, 'exit permits' and Lebanese visas became
serious problems. We were forced to stay at a hotel called the Ritz,
which was far indeed from being ritzy, except in its prices. From
the window of our room there was an excellent view of some
P.W.D. workers camped below and I enjoyed watching their
amiable idleness. The fountains too, so beloved by Persians were
a pleasure to see, playing with wild extravagance in the centre of
the roundabout beside a large statue of Reza Shah, the energetic
reformer, father of the present King of Kings. Teheran is a strange
mixture, it was much 'Westernized' by Reza Shah, and to me then
it seemed more Continental than oriental in flavour—even in
smells as well as appearance.

Reza Shah forbade camels in Teheran, but sometimes a man
on a donkey would appear making a dangerous crossing, incongruous among the smart traffic and red double-decker buses.

We mostly ate out, at a pretty little restaurant nearby in a
walled garden where the food was good. Such dishes as Caspian
sturgeon grilled with tarragon and orange, and an *hors d'oeuvres*
of Persian caviare made a welcome change. There was also a dish,
possibly of Russian inspiration, which seemed very popular, and
which we tried one day. It consisted of hot, flat pancake-like bread
called *blini* that one is supposed to eat smothered in melted butter,
with caviare, ham, smoked sturgeon and smoked herring, sandwiched with more *blini*, more butter, and lashed up with cream—
that I took to be curds, an unnecessary complication. If one avoids
the cream, it's quite a good dish although it sounds nauseating, but
after it neither of us felt we would have much need to eat for
several days.

On the Saturday we found an excellent Volkswagen agent,
where Ark was overhauled. Apparently the garage in Isfahan
had done something extraordinary to the engine timing, which
accounted for our terribly laboured progress on the road to

Teheran. After this she went like a bird and we had no further trouble. To our amazement we obtained the Lebanese visas promptly without any difficulty; now all that remained to cause delay were the 'exit permits'. For some reason it seems extremely complicated to leave Persia, even more so than to get in.

With a quartet of exotic-looking cabaret singers, we had reported at the pompous Persepolis-style Police Station (about which there is a much bandied joke—'Persé polis'), where we had been none too politely glared at by a brusque young official, and told to return at eight on Sunday morning. Being only too anxious to leave the hotel we got up very early, paid our bill, filled our water cans, packed everything into Ark, left her ready in the hotel's walled garden, and took a taxi back to the 'Persé polis'. It was an alarming ride—the driver gesticulating violently all the time while deep in conversation with his friend. The taxi had pink plastic seats, and a wallpaper of red and green leaves was plastered all over its roof. Again simultaneously with the cabaret artistes, we arrived at the police headquarters only to be sent, though quite politely this time, to yet another office, where we were told we would find our 'yellow cards', the annoying 'exit permit' that every foreigner must have.

After a prolonged search, we found this second, smaller office and were requested to wait until four or five in the afternoon. The delay was maddening; we had hoped to be camping by the Caspian Sea that night, we certainly did not want another night at the Ritz, and we were running low in funds. So, for hours we lurked in Ark in the garden among the Ritz's washing, wandering out only once to look longingly at the carpet shops. It was a long and frustrating Sunday, and when at last we were given our permits we fairly charged out of Teheran on the Karaj road, itching to be in the wilds again.

Ultimately, we were grateful to the police for the delay : had it not occurred we should have hurried over the finest pass of the entire journey. As it was we made no attempt to go far that evening, before sunset we found a wide, rock amphitheatre, a flat piece of land on an arc of the Karaj River where it hurtled down from the Elburz Mountains. We washed in the river, lit a fire and presently cooked a little supper on the bank.

A squint-eyed ruffianly-looking man came and stared, and then went likewise to wash his hands in the river. Ostentatiously, Stuart got out his biggest kukri and began to chop firewood for the volcano kettle, then as the man still lingered, began to sharpen the weapon on a stone with a flourishing touch of good showmanship.* The man soon departed, and we were left in peace, with only the sound of the Karaj roaring against its splendid curve of rock wall, and headlights of cars showing from time to time on the distant road.

I thought, as I looked at the great scooped-out wall of the river bed patterned with tiny goat tracks, and later, when it was dark, at the well of black hills around us and the starlit bowl of the night above, that we were now in what must have once been part of the sea of Gonawanaland. It was a tremendously impressive piece of country, and that camping site sent one's spirits up with a leap after the annoying frustrations of civilization in Teheran.

We both slept well, awakened with first light, and started off early on one of the most memorable drives of the trip. The Chalus is the finest pass that either of us had seen, in Europe or Asia, and although we later travelled over several magnificent passes in mountainous eastern Turkey, there was nothing as thrilling as this. It was a well-graded road, mounting slowly through typical Persian barren rocky scenery, where a few small villages added a shimmer of rose-pink fruit blossom showing through the delicate green of poplars—trees as slim as wands which every Persian village grows for fuel. The higher we mounted the bleaker it became. The road wound through rugged hunting country, hills of wild and glorious strata. Then above the great Karaj dam project—which is to save the snow water from running to waste in the salt deserts—the peaks began to draw in closer all around.

We were climbing steadily and rapidly, Ark purring along happily; presently we saw that the old road had fallen away, it lay deep in snow-drifts under a series of broken avalanche barriers; at first the new road, if indeed it were there, was not visible, it seemed that a wall of dark mountains blocked the route. Then we rounded a steep corner, and saw close at hand the road vanishing into the rock. Two lorries were drawn up waiting outside the black maw of a tunnel gaping in the mountain like the home of some huge race of troglodytes, the great, red iron sliding doors now drawn

---

* We had thought it best to carry no firearms, but we had the two kukris, a Malay dagger, and a sword-stick each, all of which gave us a certain feeling of security, and Stuart's principle of the deliberately flourished weapon invariably worked.

back. After some time the lights of an oncoming truck showed deep in the darkness, and presently with a tremendous rattle and roar a tall, typically Persian lorry appeared out of the mountain.

Then it was our turn : sandwiched between the two large trucks, and glad of their company the little van chugged up to delve into the mountain's heart, in an echoing roaring darkness. The pass is 11,000 feet above sea-level : at the crest, the din lessened as all three vehicles changed gear and went slowly down the long decline towards the Caspian side of the Elburz, with its so vastly different climate : once over the crest the whole tunnel began to stream with water from the melting snows above. Out into the sunlight again, we stopped to look back at the mountain, it was an almost sheer wall of snow.

As we dropped down, the terrain changed with incredible rapidity; there were signs of alpine verdure, small rivulet-watered alps, a few trees and herds of cows. On the steep hill-sides there were spring flowers—cowslips, scyllas and violets marking the extraordinary geographical contrasts presented by this dramatic watershed.

The road wound and twisted down to a dizzy gorge, some thousands of feet below. It dropped so steeply to the heat—an almost tropical heat with dripping mossy rocks and lizards basking in the sun—that as the crow flies the fall could not have been more than half a mile, but as the road went it was some six miles of sharp hairpin bends. It held us spellbound. After so long in the desert and the dry heat of India before the rains, it was strange and wonderful to see lavish foliage again, emerald green fields, small bright beeches, meadows full of tiny scarlet poppies. Not since we had left Malaya had we seen such a wealth of lush greenness. There were fields of green wheat sheer above the tumbling Chalus; there was the tinkle of cowbells, there were pretty, fair-skinned girls gay in red waistcoats and full skirts, there were tiny rice-fields flooded for the planting; hoopoe birds flirting across the road, and now it was so hot that we began to long for the sea and a swim.

The Caspian is a strange sea; the largest inland one in the world eighty-five feet below ordinary sea-level and it is sinking still further, partly owing to evaporation and partly, so it is said, to the Russian damming of the Volga and other rivers that flow into it, for irrigation purposes. To us it proved to be an anti-climax : through the long hot afternoon we drove along its thickly populated coastal belt, but failed to reach its sands; because marshes and paddy fields, or else wired-in building sites for the holiday bungalows of wealthy Iranians put us off. There was one 'Motel', at which the 'Indiaman' had stopped (as we learnt months later when we met the Fords again in England), but it looked so unattractive that we passed it by and thus, had we known it, lost our only chance of a Caspian swim.

After the Persia of the desert this fertile coastal belt was like another land, luxuriant with wild iris—purple and white, wisteria and mulberries; countless tortoises crossed the road, and everywhere one saw peasant women in gorgeously-coloured vivid skirts and blouses and elaborate headscarves, freer in their dress, no dust-sheet *chadar* here. This was the nearest we came to Russia, the Caucasian influence was marked, and yet incongruously a touch of tropical Asia was there too. The rice-fields at sunset recalled Malaya, and so did one or two of the hamlets with their little verandahed wooden houses, and the fishermen with their casting nets.

There were several charming little towns, where groups of women in their coloured skirts billowed along the road—not since Amritsar had we seen so much colour in dress.

In the late afternoon we turned south and away from the sea, struggling along through beautiful country on an appalling road where we developed a slow puncture. Resht greeted one with Pepsi-Cola, Tide, Kodak and Michelin advertisements and a road so ghastly that the 30 m.p.h. sign was a mockery. After Resht we looked in vain for a pull-off, there seemed no flat table anywhere for the night's camping. It was nearly dark when well beyond Resht we faced the mountains once more and still it was impossible to park.

At last at eight o'clock we found a grass verge in the dark, propped Ark up on a jack to take the weight off the slow puncture, ate a hasty meal and went to sleep, tired out by the many variations of scenery, climate and mood crammed into the last sixteen hours.

We awoke next morning to birdsong, and found we were beside fields that were almost English-looking with their buttercups and cows. Daylight also revealed a second tyre now rapidly expiring. While we were tackling it with two jacks a lorry driver waved,

slowed down in his own cloud of dust and stopped to help. Aided
by his wife, a bright sparse little woman, and his robust handy-
man, he swiftly supplied air for both tyres from a gadget run from
his engine, whipped off the wheel and changed it. So it wasn't long
before we were on the road again, now more than ever enamoured
of Persian road manners, and of Persian lorry drivers in particular.

At half-past six schoolboys began to appear, dawdling along
with their books, their bright enquiring eyes turned always to look
at Ark with interest. Rush hour on these roads lasted from then
until half-past seven, during which time we travelled in a con-
tinuous cloud of dust thrown up by buses and lorries above a
beautiful sprawling river valley stretching its many channels
among stony beds and green rice fields.

So we recrossed the Elburz that day following the vast winding
River Seefeed; it was a beautiful pass, but softer, not as dramatic
as the Chalus had been. Rush hour over, we began mounting, free
of dust now, through little stony villages of mud-topped houses
with a touch of cerulean blue at their windows, jutting out from
the hillside among olive trees, framed by the rich earth, the towering green of the hills, and the swift, mud-warm hurrying river now
far below. In one such village we stopped to have both punctures
mended. In the tyre shop, a mud and brick shack with an earth
roof, there was Persian music on the radio, the walls were decorated with countless 'pin-ups' — Ziegfield Follies, American whisky
advertisements, and Persian information posters. The smiling
green-eyed proprietor served small glasses of hot clear tea while we
waited. There was a wonderful scent of blossom; above the sound
of the mountain stream that ran through the village came the
jingle of donkey bells, and there was a little smiling boy with a
pink rose in his mouth who followed me around. As we drove
away he took the rose from his lips, and handed it to me with a
gallant flourish. Its stalk was well-chewed but the flower smelled
very sweet.

Once past the huge Seefeed Rud barrage the road descended
into barren lands again, and that night we camped in the plain
between the road and the railway, beyond Kazvin, a bleak and
depressing town that appeared to be nothing but one large rubbish dump. The next day it rained heavily, and for the first time
we lost our way and wasted three hours. We found ourselves on
an appallingly narrow mud road in a rainstorm, half way to

Hamadan in the south, when we should have been on the way to Tabriz in the north. Polite and kindly as Persian lorry drivers are, their lorries are so immense that they cannot help but splatter any small vehicle with mud, so that when Ark re-emerged on the right road again she looked as if she were made of milk chocolate. Again we camped by the railway line. It was very lonely there, but we had one visitor, a young Danish engineer on his way from Tabriz to Teheran. The effect of the *blinis* having now worn off, we cooked a large stew, enlivening it with Malacca curry powder and Savitri's chutney, and while we ate we made out a shopping list for Tabriz—the town we hoped to reach next day. It was imperative to do so for the day after was a Friday, the Sabbath again, and we needed : a new tyre, water, service, money, eggs, oranges, bread and vodka.

Here the lorries seemed taller than ever, they were lit with coloured lights, blue ones at the side like antennae, red and white headlights, and a coronet of yellow and green lamps above the driver's cab. Not only was the effect gay but it served a good purpose in outlining the size of the monster.

When we left camp next morning, the dawn was stormy and grim. The road cut into dark, snowy hills, through two long high passes and down to a wild and splendid river gorge. At last the sun came out : there were big yellow poppies and tall blu-gloss growing at the roadside above the roaring majestic river.

The day was more pleasant now, but there were still 120 miles to go to Tabriz, and some shocking wadis and wide river-beds to cross. Once again I did my bouncing act, shot off the seat and disappeared under the dashboard, while in the back my long-suffering typewriter also took another crash, on the biggest bump we'd had yet.

A blue-black storm hung over the high mountain group that hid our last Persian town. On the bleak uplands a few P.W.D. road-workers lay huddled together for their noon siesta, determined but miserable under great-coats in the endless cold rain. The air was as cold as a draught of iced wine, the sun hot. Snow lay below in the gullies, for we were mounting now above what must have been our seventh spring—but I had lost count.

Faint snow-covered mountains showed far ahead, in Turkey perhaps, and then at last we bounced into Tabriz over vast cobbles and much broken tarmac, for Tabriz is a town frequently shattered by earthquakes—as of course is much of Persia.

There was a really good garage, where service was quick and thorough. I sat working in Ark while the milk chocolate was hosed off her—an odd experience this—and by some marvellous stroke of luck we managed to buy a new heavy-duty tyre. The water was good and so we filled all the jerry cans, and while we waited friendly garage hands sent out for stamps and fresh eggs—we certainly could not have had better service. Our own shopping spree in Tabriz was also a highly successful affair, for somehow Tabriz was exhilarating, the people quick, eager and kindly. 'Tah-*breeze*' as Persians pronounce it, giving the syllables their full value, was a memorable place with its April shower weather, and its Russian air; the second largest and most elusive city in the land tucked away in all this wilderness of hills.

We camped outside in an open space that we had marked on the way in, dined sumptuously off rice and local frankfurters, and slept well through an intensely cold night. The morning's early sunlight was vivid on the twelve-thousand foot snows to the west, and Tabriz' hill was red, almost blood red lying still in shadow. As we drove again through the earthquake-torn streets we noticed that here the morning *nams* were carried on the heads of men—not as in Isfahan by little boys nibbling as they went—and were so huge that they looked like folded blankets. Perhaps it is something to do with the electric atmosphere, that only man-size *nams* will satisfy 'Tah-breeze' appetites.

There were a number of Krishna birds sitting on the telegraph wires, not flying about as they do in India, but looking cold and disconsolate. Out in the fields all alone, an old man was ploughing, and beyond him our road stretched away for miles, twisting like a little thread of dun-coloured silk, up over the plain towards the yet higher snows of eastern Turkey—the 17,000 foot Ararat itself, the volcanic cones of Kurdistan, and all the confused mountain trends, where Zagros, Elburz and Kurdish Taurus meet in the high lava uplands.

We had intended reaching the Turkish frontier that day some 190 miles on, but shortly before sunset we saw a great white peak ahead, and wondered if it could be Ararat. Then it was hidden by the shoulder of a hill, and a village in a valley was flushed suddenly with gold below a long ridge of lava, washed an incredible mul-

berry red in cloud shadow—and the temptation to stop and paint
was too strong. Later, as we turned the corner above that village,
the sudden startling beauty of Mount Ararat stopped us again
dead in our tracks. Against its two towering white cones a pair of
grazing camels stood darkly silhouetted.

This was too wonderful to pass by, and we immediately gave
up all idea of pushing on to the frontier. We soon found a flat
stony place on an old lava bed with a full view of the mountain—
a slightly sloping plateau of pumice-like rock above a deep gorge
where an unseen river thundering below sliced through the ochres
and browns of the plain, that rolled up like a sea to the ethereal
slopes of those exquisite twin cones.

The sunset colours died away on the snows, and a new moon
floated clear, high above the pass leading to the Turkish border.
This, our last camping-site in Persia, was the best of them all with
the great mountain fading slowly into the night as the stars came
out.

It was lonely here, for being so near to the frontier there were
no friendly Persian trucks rattling past, in fact there was no traffic
at all that evening. Stuart turned on the radio, and we heard from
Washington of riots in Turkey and martial law, of the terrible
earthquake at Lars in Persia, of Cheeseman's execution in the
U.S.A., and then for the first time we got London, but only for a
second or two—we realized that Russia was deliberately jamming
the B.B.C.; what we did hear typically enough was the Test match
at the Oval.

Under Ararat we had no visitors until morning. At first light
the mountain was a twin blue wraith, flushing slowly with the
dawn to pink and gold above the dark plain. A flight of pigeons
flew across above the gorge towards the rising sun, and one's
thoughts turned inevitably to Noah and the real Ark.

When it was light a smiling young shepherd came to call with
his herd, and later still a single car passed by on the road above,
a black saloon with skis lashed onto the roof. I believe that
travellers mostly sleep at Bazergan, the frontier douane.

In the gorge above which we had seen the young moon set, was
a little village called Maku, its houses like rocks jutted from the
cliff face, a bright gilded statue of the Shah stood in its single
street. There were fruit orchards vivid against the snows; there
were schoolgirls in grey dresses and red trousers, and schoolboys

waving and shouting; a pair of very fresh white horses ridden by
soldiers broke into a canter at the sight of Ark against the early sun,
and at the end of the village Persia wished us goodbye with a
'A Happy Trip' notice-board. Then there was Ararat again with
its smaller image, and we were at the frontier. Here the road runs
through a square fortress-like building that embodies both countries' Customs; in the centre of the square a Persian soldier
marches up and down one side of a low bank and a Turkish on the
other, both carrying rifles with fixed bayonets and both in tin
helmets—the Turk in a British style, the Persian in an American
style.

We gained two hours' time here, for Eastern Turkey keeps Central
European time, which made a very long day of it. We advanced
slowly then through a tremendous countryside into the military
zone of Eastern Anatolia, and for some time still the glorious shape
of Ararat was close at hand.

❖❖ 12 ❖❖

Through Eastern Anatolia

The military zone was prickly with prohibitions : no photography, no stopping, and in some places — escorts required.

But the views of Ararat were superb, its huge white cone towering above green fields and dark foothills, and it was not until later in the morning that we saw the last of the mountain, its great head veiled in cloud. It was a fine day of hot sunshine and cold wind, at the edges of hard snow-drifts beside the road small crocuses and little scyllas were thrusting their way through. We felt abundantly fit and cheerful, and the cold air made us ravenously hungry.

Turkish women wore no veils, their full-skirted dresses and bound-around head gear were attractive, many of them wandered along spindle in hand like the women of Greece. There were no more lorries, there was scarcely any traffic on the roads except for a few jeeps. In the fields oxen were dragging the ploughs, many of the labourers wore thick fur-collared jackets. High snows lay all around, and dark snow clouds lingered on many of the peaks.

In every village darkly-dressed men filled the streets, they must have been discussing the riots, and the revolution that was even then taking place in Ankara and Istanbul; obviously every man jack of them had downed tools that day. They were animated and excited, and they pressed around us eagerly but we could only gesture and smile. At one village where we stopped for petrol I was almost mobbed while Stuart was unlocking the tank, but they were smiling and friendly, and seemed pleased to know that we were English.

Some of the people were quite fair, with blond fresh faces. The minarets were needle tall, spiky, phallic, typically Byzantine, utterly different from the bosom-domed ones of Persia.

Apart from the High Chalus, and that brief hail storm on the pass above Isfahan this was our first real winter of the drive; there was not a tree in leaf. There were no more mud houses, but grim stone villages, filled with handsome, red-lipped men with ruddy cheeks and bright green eyes. Great fingers of melting snow stained red with earth sprawled over dark green and black hills, and the rivers were swollen, hurrying with the snow waters.

After a place called Agri the road climbs to a pass 10,000 feet above sea-level. It was snowing here, and drifts lay down to the road and below it in the gullies, we crawled up in bottom gear to the col. In the true winter this road is kept open by snow ploughs, and we thought of the three Australians whom we had met in Gwalior who said they had slept in huts with the snow plough men. We paused at the top to fill our jerry cans with cold fresh water at a spring gushing out of the mountain.

It was here that we began to see those great grey dogs that are so common in this area, said to be Salukis, but they are not as slim as the Salukis we know, they are more like small lions with the colouring of Siamese cats and a crazy penchant much encouraged by their shepherd owners, for chasing any moving vehicle. They are magnificent dogs, but trained as they are from puppyhood to race cars, unfortunately many of them get killed.

Coming down towards Pasliner there was a man standing upright in his cart as if it were a chariot, and galloping his pair of horses over the dark plain. We were nearing the strict military zone, and at Pasliner had to take on an armed escort to Erzerum about twenty-four miles ahead. A handsome, dashing young man in an immaculate uniform, he was obviously overcome with boredom. I felt painfully conscious of our gypsy-like appearance beside his spotless one.

Whether we wanted to or not we were forced to stay in Erzerum that night, for our passports were taken from us, our polite and well-groomed escort took us to an hotel where we were expected to stay—there appeared to be no choice—a dim, overheated place smelling of sulphur. We were informed that our passports would be returned at eight o'clock the following morning.

As we came into the town I had had an impression of tall minarets and earth-coloured domes stark against the snows and the sunset, and then it was dark—and it was very dark in Erzerum indeed. It was like walking into a Dostoevsky novel : there were droshkies sliding down cobbled streets between drab, sour smelling walls, heaps of earth and rubble, soldiers everywhere, women wrapped in sacking-like garments, a tiny wooden shop selling raki, cigarettes and spring onions. Dim and candle-lit, nothing seemed quite real to me that night : at the restaurant off the steep cobbled street where we dined, we both felt as if we had stepped into the past, although the building was modern. We were ushered into the kitchen to choose our dinner straight off the hob; braised mutton, pilaff and vegetables — we were ravenously hungry after the long cold day, and it tasted good, accompanied by a bottle of some nameless but palatable and warming red wine.

It seemed a womanless world, for apart from myself and one other female traveller the restaurant was crowded with men.

A strange, mysterious unlovable town — we locked up Ark very carefully, there was nowhere to put her except in a small gap beside the hotel. Then we climbed numerous flights of stairs in the gloom and took a welcome scalding hot bath in a scruffy bathroom with no lock on the door. Eventually I slept, only to wake to blazing sunlight at four a.m. Used as we were to rising with the first light, I cussed the Eastern Turkish habit of keeping Central European time, it would be four hours at least before we could retrieve our passports. While waiting outside the police station later, we met two young Persian travellers returning to Iran, who had more alarming tales — of Turkish roads ahead, and of gangs of stone-throwing boys and men. These young Persians after years abroad were deeply depressed by the backwardness of Turkey, and now they had begun to dread seeing their own country, for fear that they would find it also dirty and backward in contrast with Europe. They seemed quite pathetically heartened when we said we had been made happy in Persia, and had liked it so well.

Once free of Erzerum we discovered that the Turkish county-side was both varied, and beautiful, almost any of the valleys would rival those of Switzerland, and yet all were supremely lonely and unexploited. If we had not been nervous of Turkey and rather worried by the possible effects of the present revolution — of which we had no further news at all — we might have lingered there with the utmost delight. This glimpse was particularly tantalizing, it was like leaving a great feast untasted.

That day we encountered our first 'predatory' Kurds. If anything their appearance is even more impressive than that of the Afghans. We were extremely fortunate to see both peoples on the march up to their summer pastures : with the Afghans we had been travelling in the same direction, with the Kurds of course the position was reversed, for we were going down to the plains from the high uplands. The Kurds have lived their semi-nomadic existence in this part of the world for well over four thousand years. They are not true nomads, as are the Bedouin, but like the Afghans they are really pastoral people practising transhumance. Fisher says that their mode of life seems scarcely to have varied since they occupied their present homeland in 2400 B.C., and 'that they have claims to racial purity and to continuity of culture that are stronger than those of any European nation', but in 'a limited sense, for the Kurds are renowned as a fierce and predatory people, and their social organization has not progressed beyond the level of tribal grouping.'

The women wore full skirts over long red trousers, their mouths bound across with white cloths against the dust, their faces red-dark, clean-cut, with eyes like turquoises, and they sat their frisky ponies as if born to them. Some of the women looked as tough and as weather-beaten as the men, and others were beautiful and vivid, with flaming red hair and challengingly fierce blue eyes; often they wore elaborate ornaments dangling over their tightly-bound brows.

That day we descended into what must have been our eighth or ninth spring, we were in the Armenian Highlands now. The next range of mountains that we were approaching was the Kurdish Taurus, running in an arc from Malayta on the west towards the Western Zagros range in the east.

That first night we had some difficulty in avoiding the herds, and camped at last only just off the road; it was dark by the time we started cooking, and almost immediately we received a visit from three extremely tough-looking soldiers. Having heard spine-chilling stories of the rape of both sexes by soldiers in Turkey I loosened my sword in its stick;* while Stuart, his kukri on his hip, bent over the fire outside and managed to appear quite unconcerned. With the three huge men in rough battle-dress standing around him, he looked horribly defenceless. The soldiers accepted cigaretttes, but for some time it seemed as if they could not make up their minds about us; one swung a grappling iron in his hand,

* Had we, instead of listening to such tales, been able to read Freya Stark's opinion of Turkish manners in her *Alexander's Path* before we reached Turkey, we would even more quickly have come to the conclusions that we rapidly drew for ourselves, nevertheless, and would have rightly disregarded as trash those other evidently worthless accounts.

Jerash, Jordan : (*above*) the elliptical forum and (*below*) the Roman ruins with the hills of Gilead in the background

Petra, South Jordan: (*above*) weather-worn tombs carved in the multi-coloured sandstone wall of the north-eastern face; (*below*) the rosy El Khazneh rising from a sea of red oleanders

and another held a coil of rope. After a little while they moved a yard or two away, tapped the telegraph wire and proceeded to send a message—about us perhaps, and having decided that we were harmless enough, they saluted politely and left us to sleep in peace.

We were off early the next morning, but even then we were not on the road much before the Turkish boys, who were on their way to school at 4.45 a.m. In Pertek, the first village we came to, we found shops open at five o'clock, a woman in ballooning trousers was already busy washing the windows of her cottage, and a waiter with a tray of tea glasses was running across a little green garden full of flowers and fountains. It seems that country Turks are very early risers.

At seven o'clock we stopped to buy fresh bread and raki. Now we were almost into our Baedeker, 'Palestine and Syria', published in 1894. It proved invaluable in the next five and a half weeks that we spent in the area.

The road followed the great Firat (Euphrates) River most of that day. It was a pleasant road bounded with little fir trees, and rich fertile valleys on either hand, for we were coming down rapidly into the Fertile Crescent, and now we both longed to reach the Mediterranean. Certainly the climatic changes that we experienced on this day's drive were again most dramatic; from drab winter snows, to hot summer and ripe wheat, a warm scent of hay, and white laburnum blossom.

Everywhere the Kurds were on the move with their black tents, their red and white ponies, dark camels and bright washing, and their children in scarlet scattered on the sunlit shoulder of a hill among masses of blue and yellow wild flowers.

That evening, again avoiding the herds we camped in a little valley, brilliantly carpeted with blu-gloss, poppies, clover, and some bright yellow flowers; it was a shallow vale between two hills with a sheen of wild wheat among the flowers. Only one man passed by, a broad-shouldered fellow walking very fast at dusk, and he called out in a ringing voice : *'Sala'am alaikum!'*

'Wa'alaikum as-sala'am!' Stuart called back.

In that flowery meadow Stuart switched on the radio, and voices poured forth, of this country and of others, and it seemed then for a while as if all the world lay before me, and yet so tantalizingly it was not within my grasp; for all too soon I would

I

be anchored down again in one small spot, and the infectious
'*snobisme du desert*' would no longer be ours.

The Prophet said : 'A plough is never taken into the house without baseness going in also'—meaning that one cannot lead a
settled life without some of the mud and sludge of the field invad-
ing the house, and the mind also; the proud spiritual and physical
freedom of nomadic pastoral life inevitably is destroyed by a
settled one.

It was somewhere about here that the full impact of this pastoral way of life began to be forced upon us both, and the further
south we went from now on and in Jordan above all, so the Bible
and particularly the Old Testament, began to come alive with
new meaning and reality.

Next morning, we awoke at half-past three to the lowing of a
herd, and looking out of the window we saw that Ark was completely surrounded by flowing woolly backs. It was still not really
light; we lay silent and watched the herds, driven by two men and
four dogs, retreat and divide well up the hillside before we got out
to brew our tea among the vivid flowers. Those herds gave me new
confidence : the men could so easily have banged on the side of
Ark, to ask for cigarettes or to annoy us, but they did nothing,
merely streamed by, quietly going their way in peace. Why are
there so many fearsome travellers' tales? Were we only lucky, or
was it not that what we experienced was the more general way of
life, a natural give and take between nomads whether they be on
the hoof, or on the wheel? But as the sky grew rapidly lighter I
kept my eyes on those four big grey dogs : they were watching our
movements with interest and slowly they began edging down the
hillside on their bellies—no doubt waiting for the engine to start
up when Ark would immediately become fair game.

The Kurds are a vivid exciting-looking people about whom I
should love to know more. The whole of the ensuing morning we
passed through groups of them with their herds going north; the
red hair and blue eyes of many suggests a Nordic element. Their
colouring is superb—darkly rosy faces contrasting with light eyes
and bright hair. Their curly-headed babies, bound like those of
the Afghans on top of camels, were warmly wrapped in blankets,
their little dark, blond or rusty-red heads all abob. Other babies
bulged like puppies from the ponies' saddlebags, two small blond
boys rode one pony, their pet lambs tucked into the saddlebags at

their knees. Some of the children were beautiful : many of the women spinning as they walked led their camels and donkeys, while the baby camels as soft as velvet bounded along behind. An old, old woman with a proud, shut, matriarchal face rode a donkey as if it were a war horse; a lovely blonde girl in a dress of Reckitts blue was dwarfed by the restive camel she fearlessly controlled. There were not many men to be seen, but the few young ones were remarkably good to look at, the old men, who wore long white beards, were patriarchal and intensely alert. Presumably the younger men were mostly ahead, pasturing some of the herds, while the women packed up camp and moved the rest. As we progressed further south and west we encountered fewer and fewer of these colourful nomads and began to meet the more sophisticated peoples of the coastal strip. So through Antioch, and on — up the long grind of the steep Mons Cassius pass. At the Syrian frontier we were allowed through only after a rather petulant official had expunged the word 'Israel' from one of our maps.

We were now longing to reach the Mediterranean; to bathe and to tidy a little before going on into the Lebanon, where the welcome of relatives awaited us, and the civilization and the flesh-pots of Beirut.

⋙ 13 ⋘

Friendly Jordan

We lotus ate in the Lebanon for six days, and on the seventh we were ready to set off once more for — Ba'albek, Jerash, Jerusalem, Petra at last, and, possibly, Akaba on the Red Sea.

After two blue sun-filled and windy days exploring Ba'albek and painting there, we turned south again.

There was snow on Mount Hermon. This range, with the Anti-Lebanon, guards the gateway into Syria, and the road to Damascus one of the few east-west cuts that breaks across the great parallel north-south rifts.

Through barren hills the road came suddenly down into the thickly grown green cleft of El Ghouta, watered by the Barada, which means cold, but which the Greeks called The Golden Stream. We did not plan to go into Damascus that day but afterwards, when we did, I came to think that this oasis of El Ghouta, the garden of Damascus was the town's most attractive feature. In this narrow *V* of foliage of walnuts and pomegranates below the brown desert hill there were gaily-painted outdoor restaurants enticing in the sunshine of the green gorge. Many of the cafés were built out on small stilt-supported platforms above waterfalls, and I longed to stop, but we knew that a stretch of bad desert road was to come, and that we must keep going if we wanted to reach Jordan before dark. We began singing :

> One more river to Jordan,
> One more river to cross.

In this part of the world there *always* seems to be one more river or one more wadi to cross.

I started reading up again about Jerash : it was founded about 300 B.C., once one of the towns belonging to the Decapolis of Peraea and known then as Gerasa it was, in A.D. 117, one of the largest and strongest in Arabia, an important caravan centre in the mountains of Gilead on the inland route from Petra to Damascus, and 'a fine representative of the Romano-Syrian culture of the region.'*

It was an outpost on the very edge of the Roman Empire; once a Nabataean caravan centre; later, after the fall of Rome, a Christian town, captured in the seventh century by the Arabs; and now a little Circassian-Jordanian village.

After a short encounter with a handsome red-capped Syrian policeman, who wanted to see our passports, we turned due south heading for Jerash. The road became increasingly bad. The long dark tents of the nomads stood braced against the wind in a wild, rust-red landscape. Once again we marvelled at the extent of the Roman Empire, and at its legions toiling out here, on foot and in chariots, far from home.

There were a few fields of miserably poor wheat in this plain of red stones; how it struggled to grow at all was hard to imagine, for there were no signs of irrigation. Some huge black and white cranes flew ponderously over the scanty fields, and those scraggy-looking fowls—the white vulture, the neophron or 'Pharaoh's chickens'. We were nearing the Jordanian frontier—the Hashemite Kingdom of Jordan—to give it its full sonorous title, and I began an attempt to tidy up in the rather unlikely hope of mollifying officialdom—if needs be.

We stopped for petrol, and I was immediately assailed by a bevy of predatory and unlovely little Syrian boys all angrily trying to sell me eggs and live pigeons and soft drinks. An appalling stink of oily antiquated garlic suddenly filled the car. I could not believe that even such importunate and scruffy children could possibly exude so considerable an amount of garlic. I mentioned it to Stuart, but he had been busy with the petrol and had not noticed.

At the Syrian douane the ghastly odour persisted. Stuart returned from the office much amused, for at each frontier that day —Arabs are certainly more outspoken than Persians—he had been asked : 'Is she your *friend* or—your wife?'

As each official learnt that I was indeed Stuart's wife he had replied : 'Ah—madame *is* your wife—good! good!'

But I had not been so amused; surrounded by eggs and live pigeons and grubby hands thrusting bottles at me. 'Have a drink, *Madame*? Coca-cola, *Madame*! . . . *madame*! . . . MADAME!'

* From an Antique Land, Sir Julian Huxley.

Patience almost came to an end at times and I longed to be out of Syria.

Four frontiers in one day, and yet so poor a mileage; after the miles of Persian desert, and the vast distances of Turkey this seemed so small, the petty human barriers too close and futile. The more one journeyed the worse these seemed—barriers of language, and of State with their bureaucracy, their religious and international hatreds.

Then the Holy Land stretched away ahead, blankly red and ochre in the afternoon light, and we passed through the last Syrian barrier where little Syrian boys still pestered with Coca-cola and Seven-up, and where a fat woman in black stood under the red, white and green-starred flag of Syria shouting and yelling—giving vent to protest, perhaps, against some tedious detail of officialdom.

The Jordanian frontier: a young soldier on duty, in a red *khaffiyeh* with gilt badges above his brow; a great many camels waiting at the roadside, a little flat-roofed town rising out of the desert. . . .

We had not been in Jordan more than fifteen minutes before we began to learn something of its friendly ways. We had drawn off onto a flat pebbly bit of desert, a hundred yards or so from the road, and were starting to investigate the garlic odour, when a young man in a black and white *khaffiyeh* circled off the road on his motor-cycle and came to offer assistance. This was more like Persia: we began to feel at home. We tried to assure him that we were perfectly happy, and that nothing was wrong, we were glad to be in Jordan and had planned to camp here for the night.

'You must *please* come to my house? You cannot stay here,' he insisted. 'The militia will disturb you.'

He was charming, with a highly intelligent sensitive face. He was a schoolmaster, he told us, studying Arabic and English literature. Nothing, he said, would please him more than for us to go to his house. He was so pressing, his manner so kind that we felt bound to accept. He was on his way into the little town with an enlarged photograph of El Khazneh in Petra, which he had taken himself on a recent visit, so of course we talked about Petra and our own plans, then he promised to return shortly and guide us to his village.

While he was gone we had a raki each and straightened things up in Ark. The sun was beginning to set; we were tired and not feeling sociable, but the kindness and genuineness of the young man was so appealing, it had been impossible to refuse. Now that the van was static the garlic stench was worse than ever, and then at last I tracked it down.

'There it is!' I exclaimed. 'You put it up on the roof two nights ago!'

'What—?' said Stuart. 'Oh, yes—*so* I did!'

It was the little carton of creamed garlic which the Rue Bliss 'rosted chicken' shop issued with its hot chickens; balanced in the gutter over the doorway, we'd bought it four days ago in Beirut—no wonder the Ark stank!

The schoolmaster returned presently, and we followed his neat figure on the motor-cycle into the desert, his *khaffiyeh* flying under its rakish black head cords. The long grey road wound into the blue hills, and to the west the sky was red above the dark red earth. Then in the distance the lights of a little village began to glitter between the swarthy earth and the indigo clouds.

His name was Abdul Rahman, a name very familiar to us in Malaya, being that of our friend, her first Paramount Ruler, and also of her Prime Minister. This Jordanian Abdul Rahman had a shy, handsome young wife, and a lovely three-year-old daughter with bright eyes and darkly golden hair.

I was doing some drawings in the bedroom—where we all sat warmed by the heat of two oil lamps—when neighbours called with their baby—a cheerful plump woman in a purple velvet gown and a tall man with a humorous bony face framed in his flowing *khaffiyeh*. For some reason, I think to fetch a book that they wished to see, Stuart and I went out to Ark. I returned first—the tall man was doubled up, head down on a mat half across the door, while the others sat in silence in the lamplight, the babies lying rolled in swaddling clothes like twin cocoons on the bed. I hesitated; it seemed a funny place and time to choose for prayer, however, after a suitable pause I tip-toed round behind him. At once there was a shriek of joy, and the big man leapt up, so full of congratulations that I thought he was about to embrace me, and everyone burst out laughing: I had passed the test.

Abdul Rahman was apologetic, he had been unable to prevent this trick being played on me; devised by the women, it was to discover whether I possessed the right kind of manners and could keep a straight face at the sight of the prostrate form on the mat.

I was most amused : luckily I'd lived long enough in a Muslim country and although surprised I wouldn't have dreamt of laughing. After that we got on better than ever, now we were fully accepted, by the women as well as by the men.

Presently Abdul Rahman went to cook supper for us himself — after the meal we washed perfunctorily under the tap on the verandah, and saw the moon rising red over the plain. They rather wanted us to sleep in the house, but our beds in Ark were close at hand. So when we were ready and in our sleeping-bags they came to say goodnight, looking handsome in their white cotton sleeping clothes, with their shining dark eyes in smiling faces, and they lingered talking for some time in Ark's doorway against the dark well of the night and the stars above, our little oil lamp casting a warm light and deep shadows on their two comely faces.

In the morning he came early with Arab coffee, and he insisted on taking away our lamp which he had noticed was dirty, and he cleaned it himself. In fact he seemed to do everything for us himself, and later when we were up and dressed it was he again who cooked the breakfast. Besides Arabic and English he spoke some Hebrew and was learning French, and he was already teaching English to his little daughter. Quite clearly he doted on her, and she was very beautiful with that sun-touched golden curling hair above her creamy complexion and warm light brown eyes. She was entranced with Ark's mascot — 'Ararat' — whose voice now was becoming hoarse with use.

The breakfast was of eggs, unleavened bread, olive oil, goat's cheese and Arab coffee. A dark, thin little servant maid who appeared later, looked like a Bedouin; she was childishly pleased with some sweets that I gave her and also delighted by 'Ararat' — but then she was only ten years old.

Over the door of the house there was written in Arabic script : 'Thanks be to God who gave me enough money to build this house.'

Abdul Rahman was shortly to take another English language examination in Damascus, but he would be here when we returned from Petra and Akaba, and he begged us to call in again. Before we left he warned us to be careful how we photographed the Bedouin; he said they were inclined to dislike 'rich foreigners taking photographs as they think they go away and publish them abroad saying the Arabs are cannibals, as a form of anti-Islamic propaganda. . . .' I wondered whence came this idea, but he could not explain—Israel perhaps?

In Jordan just as they say 'GOOd—gOOd' with attractive emphasis on the oo sound, so do they say 'Well-*come*!' Abdul Rahman had given us a very happy welcome to Jordan, and the same sense of kindness and friendliness lasted throughout our journey there. My love for Jordan, the Holy Land, increased daily, and above all the countries we saw—I think it is Jordan to which I would most like to return. Not since India had we met with such hospitality.

We saw a great many Bedouin that day as we came down towards Jerash's golden brown ruins among the green and brown hills, the poplars and the figs. And Circassians too, in gleaming black silks and velvets as dark as ravens against the temples and pale sun-baked sand. Jerash was a wonderful setting for these handsome people, who passed to and fro among the ruins, regardless of the vivid effect they created against such a background. A man and a boy, with their herd of black goats; a graceful swarthy girl mounted on a donkey moving leisurely across in front of the forum leading a string of black bulls to pasture—each group a separate frieze of raven glossy shapes contrasting superbly with the warmth of sunlit Ionic stone.

In Jerash we had another friendly encounter. There is nowhere to stay in the village—not that this worried us—but when we had walked around a little we met the guardian of the antiquities, Ahmat Shistewa, a smiling young man with the darkly ruddy complexion of the outdoor Arab. He was not a trained archaeologist, but he had been on many of the Antiquities Department expeditions to Petra—which he knew well—and he loved his work here in Jerash. Would we not like to sleep the night here on the little terrace above the stream, so that we might see the forum by the light of the full moon? Naturally we accepted promptly.

That afternoon the Roman street was hot and balmy, only lizards basked on the earthquake-riven stones where chariot wheels had scored deep ruts. These are wonderful ruins; the unique elliptical forum, the long colonnaded street, the tetrapylon, and the theatres. The little theatre is one of the most perfect classical theatres one could hope to see; deserted and baking hot in these sun-filled hills of Gilead. As we climbed up the long flight of steps to the ruined Christian church, where there once stood a temple to the infant Dionysius, the muezzin's call to prayer began ringing out from the little village below : *'La ilaha ila Allah taala!'* and it continued to sound until we had reached the top, so adding a newer note—the Islamic one—to this confusion of pagan and Christian ideologies in ancient Jerash.

The terrace upon which we were to camp was alongside Ahmat Shistewa's tiny office, and we backed Ark in beside a fallen acanthus capital, which made a good camp seat. Immediately below the terrace was a tiny stream hurrying through a green grove of big spreading walnut trees—alive with birds—and pomegranate trees were in flower outside Ark's windows. Under the trees was a little tea garden managed by a fair smiling, cross-eyed Circassian boy and a retired Arab soldier. We invited our new friend Ahmat Shistewa to the Ark and were about to cook supper when he said : no, indeed, *he* would cook the meal, so we went down to the tea garden to invade the old soldier's little kitchen.

'I'm very gOOd at making omelettes,' said Ahmat Shistewa.

And indeed he was; the fair cross-eyed boy and the old man looked on amazed, and the boy kept repeating 'gOOd-gOOd' as Arabs so often do, in lieu of their own *'Qwayis-Qwayis!'*—which is also an expression of warm approval.

When we had finished eating, and Ahmat had gone home, Stuart and I went up again to the forum. This forum, and indeed most of Jerash are more perfect than any Roman ruins of the kind even in Italy. Despite earthquakes this town has withstood the centuries better than most, for it was not ransacked by house-building local people, lying at is does in Bedouin country—the dwellers in the black tents having no need of masonry—so it has been preserved in much of its pure beauty for well over two thousand years. It was not until the persecuted Circassians came to Jerash in the last century that people other than tent dwellers lived in the area.

Under the light of the rising moon all the dogs and donkeys of Jerash had gone mad, it seemed, judging from the crescendo of barking and braying that went on. But there was no man nor beast in that great elliptical forum. We had it to ourselves, and we were impressed beyond measure with the majesty and beauty of Rome. The long pavement curved below lines of slender Ionic columns; the easterly columns cast shadows that stretched three-quarters of the way across the glorious concentric pattern of the flagstones, and slowly as the moonlight strengthened, the reddish brown of the hills began to glow beyond the western columns. We lay down on the Roman paving stones, listening to the dogs and those wonderfully expressive Middle Eastern donkeys, and gazing at the shadows of the Ionic stone. Never again, I felt sure, would we have a Roman forum—and *such* a forum—in the full glory of a moonlight night entirely to ourselves.

We walked a little way then up the colonnaded street, wondering about the Romans who had built this so beautiful little provincial town far from Rome, what had their feelings been in this distant land, and how deeply they must have impressed the caravans of Nabataeans and Syrians.

It was too beautiful to go to bed: nobody—no police, no Bedouin—only this moonlit vision of ancient Rome, and a sadness, an ineffable sense of loss and waste.

In the morning I sat on the broken Corinthian capital beside Ark above the walnut trees, and watched two elegantly helmeted Jordanian policemen apparently at play with three silky black sheep in the ruins below the Temple of Zeus. Presently the sheep scampered down into Ahmat's office, rushed through it, upsetting a tray of tea glasses, and—the policemen still in pursuit—charged down the steps to the little green garden below; perhaps in search of a comrade which had just been sold, no doubt for *shish kebab*, to the cross-eyed Circassian boy.

Arab music now tinkled out from under the walnut trees; and Ahmat Shistewa came to wish us good-morning. There was, he said, to be an Army Day festival honoured by the King's presence on May 26th here in the forum, could we return for it? He would obtain permission from the Department of Antiquities in Amman. We said that of course we should be only too delighted and would make a point of returning from Akaba in time.

The day was warm and clear, and we drove on through the lovely hilly countryside of Gilead, with its little oaks, tall anchusa, a few cypresses, stunted firs, some gnarled olives and flocks of goats on the mountain as black and thick as the beloved's hair—balm in Gilead!

The rivers we crossed to the Jordan that day were limned with deep pink oleander bushes in full flower. Presently we came to the River Jabbock, red with flowers, a stream of blossom, the hot honey and almond scent of the oleanders was heavy on the air.

'Jacob rose up that night and took his two wives and his two women servants and his eleven sons and passed over the ford Jabbock. And he took them and sent them over the brook, and sent over what he had. And Jacob was left alone. . . .'*

'. . . Jacob was a plain man dwelling in tents'—exactly as the Bedouin today, the black tents of Kedar. This was the pastoral region where he reared his flocks; and it was at this brook that he overcame his distress, while Rachel and Leah waited patiently on the opposite bank.

Today on the bridge above the brook Jabbock stood two Arabs, their grinning African servant beside them. Then a man on a white horse rode out of the red oleanders and crossed the brook—just as Jacob must have done when he had wrestled with the angel, and afterwards crossed over to his people.

Out of all this scarcely touched land we came suddenly to the new American road that leads down to the Dead Sea, and its advertisements for radios, cars, shoes and brassieres jarred incongruously with a background of little, Biblical-looking villages, and the long black caterpillars of tents sprawled on the dry hillsides. We began coming down then to the River Jordan from Es Salt.

It was the season of foals : all Bedouin donkeys are enchanting, especially the foals, they prance like fawns skittishly; their dark pricked-up ears make a crescent-shaped halo above their heads. At birth the tips of their ears are lightly stitched together and kept so for three weeks, which is apparently what gives the Bedouin donkey his peculiarly perky appearance.

At Mediterranean sea-level it suddenly became very hot; the road plunged on down and down into the scorching dry barren land of the Rift, where the Jordan flows into the Dead Sea.

We stopped at the Dead Sea 'lido' hotel, in some curiosity to see such a building on the edge of so unlikely a shore.

It seemed an anomaly and we wanted to get on to Jerusalem, and yet there is something about the Dead Sea that both fascinates and repels—the oily black and white stones, the clinging leaden water. We ordered cold drinks, and sat for a little white watching elegant clerics of various nationalities walking on the verandah, and religious parties bathing unsinkably in the warm greasy sea.

* Genesis 32, 24.

At 1,490 feet below sea level, it is so salt that, as Baedeker drily says—'the human body can only be submerged with difficulty.'

We left the 'lido' gladly to continue on towards Jerusalem. The road climbed up steeply from the grim depths, through pale barren hills among which the long black 'tents of hair' of the Bedouin stood like slim ejaculations.

We were driving due west now, the evening sun full in our eyes, and yet there were still one or two visions of the jewel blue Dead Sea lying in its subfusc golden pink haze far below. Then the tall spire of the Chapel of the Ascension on the Mount of Olives appeared ahead.

There must be many thousands of people who long above all to see Jerusalem. But although we did want to see it, we were apprehensive of what we would find—disillusion, disappointment, dirt, beggars, mercenary exploitation.

We were tired, and neither of us was feeling too fit, so we went to the first hotel that had a free room. As in Benares we felt that here in Jersualem a guide was essential. So, the next morning we obtained the services of a plump young Muslim—an official guide from a tourist bureau in the New City, and—fully prepared to be disillusioned—we set off, leaving Ark at the Gate of St. Stephen in the walls of the Old City. We need not have worried; Jerusalem was clean and in many ways extremely beautiful, its bazaar full of bustling life and colour, there were no baksheesh boys nor were we pestered to buy frippery religious curios, and certainly something of what we saw must have been at least a little as it was in the days of Christ.

We walked into the Old City, passed through the house of St Anne, and looked down at the Pool of Bethesda. Perhaps one of the most interesting things about the Pool was that its story is written in no less than 132 languages set up in a porch nearby—including Malay, Batak, Shan, Cornish, Gaelic, and—among other more obscure tongues—Nias; from India alone there were twelve. Then we toiled up the Via Dolorosa, and although it is hard to credit the exact siting of the stations of the Cross, the street impressed and moved me more than I had expected. In itself it was beautiful: roses and great passion flowers hung over the grey walls of the flagellation. A student twirling a passion flower in his hand suddenly smiled and reached out to give it to Stuart as he passed by. The site of Pilate's Palace and the ruins of it that remain were brilliant too with flowers of all kinds, and small orange trees in ripe fruit grew on the terrace above the Muslim boys' school which its walls now house.

We had to leap to one side as a taxi shot up the steep hill, incongruous here but the side alleys, the little donkeys laden with stones coming steeply down on their small delicate hooves, and much else besides, must have been the same in Christ's day.

At the sixth station of the Cross, outside the Convent of the Little Sisters, was a dark shop, a deep place beautiful in its simplicity, selling bread and arak. At the cross roads was the seventh station, and many more little shops; Arabs, and veiled women in purple robes; a scent of Arab coffee and cardoman. These vivid *souks* led the eye down long vistas on either hand.

We lunched here in an Arab restaurant with a fine arched roof, on a pilaff of rice, stuffed vine leaves and aubergines. There were some good-looking Jordanian soldiers in their red *khaffiyeh*, and in one corner a peasant family, who chose to eat behind a screen, which was put around their table as if it were a hospital bed. I wondered if it was perhaps the presence of infidels that called for this protection. The guide was a long time returning from his meal, and when he arrived we went up to the Church of the Holy Sepulchre.

So much has been written about Jerusalem by others more knowledgeable than I, that I am not attempting to do more than to record my own impressions fleetingly. We were both horrified—as many have been—by this strange dim church, with its melée of Christian sects. At the gaudy lamp-hung tomb were two priests—a tall Armenian in a gold hat, and a splendid bearded Egyptian Coptic. A fair, long-haired Greek Orthodox priest submitted placidly to being flattened against the wall when the guide flung open a door literally in his face, to reveal for our benefit the original rock of the tomb.

In the maze of chapels and high-raftered roofs there came continuously on the incense-laden air the sound of chanting voices of unseen friars.

After the elaborately curtained, dark cinnabar and gold of the Roman Catholic chapel, the Crusaders' chapel of the French transition style, was simple and pleasing, shafted then with dust beams of sunlight from high above.

But the whole is an overwhelming conglomeration. The final

and of course well-known irony being that the keys of the holiest building in Christendom are held by Muslim guards, who lounge on a kind of raised ottoman at the main entrance, ready for trouble with a telephone at hand that is said to be connected directly to the police station.

After the oppressive sectarian chaos of this church we felt in need of a long, cool and strengthening drink. So the guide led the way up to a little bar in the Christian street, looking down towards the barrier of Israel, and there we rested and recovered.

Next we walked along under the Wailing Wall on the very edge of forbidden Israel territory, where there was only a rabble of children playing noisy games and dancing the cha-cha to tin can music among a handful of tourists—for the Jews are gone, and the famous way seems now to be nothing but a sort of hop-scotch alley.

Then the guide took us up to the Dome of the Rock, where one's sense of reality and the truth of fundamental religion—so dimmed in the Church of the Sepulchre with its bickering sects— is properly restored. The Haram-es-Sheref was to me the most wonderful place in Jerusalem.

David chose this high rock when he first took the land from the Jebus, and it was here that Solomon built his temple, and for a while it is said that the rock became the shelter for the Ark of the Covenant.

Today from this beautiful platform of the Haram one looks across at Israel a stone's throw away and sees how tragically the Holy City is divided; a bitter situation indeed.

The present Dome of the Rock, the Mosque of Omar, was built 1,100 years ago; it is a wonderful building, combining the best of Byzantine, Persian and Arabian architecture. It is said that the Crusaders at first presumed it to be the temple of Solomon, and it became the inspiration of several Knights Templar churches in England and in France—notably of course the Temple Church in London—all of the same octagonal structure.

Unfortunately, the interior of the mosque was being cleaned and restored, so we could not fully appreciate its wonder, but we could admire the jewel-like seventh century stained glass, and marvel at the painted wooden ceiling created by seventeenth century Indian craftsmen, recalling to us frescoes of the same period at Orcha.

Much of the interior was crowded with sacking protection and scaffolding, and we could only walk around the great Rock—the high windy threshing floor of the Jebus. We went down into the cave hollowed out below the Rock itself, whence the Prophet was said to have ascended to heaven on his miraculous steed. Here it is said also that Jesus was able to decipher the sacred unspeakable name of God—'Shem'. And here too it is believed, as in Delphi and other sanctuaries of this kind that there is below a rushing subterranean torrent sometimes to be heard, and—according to some Muslims—the Rock hovers over the abyss without support. The only relic of the Christian period, when the Crusaders converted the temple into a church in the twelfth century is the wrought iron screen which they set up to enclose the sacred Rock on which they had placed their altar.

In this strange, hollow little crypt I felt as though we stood in the very matrix of three of the world's greatest religions. To Islam now the Rock is second only in holiness to the Ka'ba at Mecca.

We came out onto the terrace to look down at the sealed Golden Gates of Jerusalem, and across the Kidron to the Garden of Gethsemane and the little blue domes of Mary Magdalen's church below the Mount of Olives. To the south-west was the pointed cone of Mount Zion, now in forbidden territory. Then we walked down to the slightly lower courtyard where splendid ilex trees stood dark besides the pool of El Kas, once fed by the pools of Solomon, in front of the eighth century mosque of El Aksa. There is something intensely pleasing about this mosque; it is light, spacious, thickly carpeted with rugs, it has height and airiness, and a true sense of practised, workaday religion and worship, and of religions older than Islam too—a feeling which is not unfounded, for the original building was a basilica erected by Justinian in honour of the Virgin Mary. At that moment, slanting sunlight shone on gorgeous seventh century glass at the south end, jewelled glass of colours unbelievably dark and rich—peacock, sapphire, pure viridian, with touches of ox-blood red and topaz above the prayer niche. As I moved away from the *mehrab* towards the east the glass looked almost as if it were opaque in the rays of the setting sun, and yet gloriously luminous as water does over coral depths flecked with light.

There was a constantly reiterated clatter, as worshippers flung

The Mount of Olives seen from the old city of Jerusalem

The Krak des Chevaliers in Syria known to the Muslims as 'The Mountain'

The courtyard and battlements of Krak des Chevaliers

their shoes into wooden boxes beside the pillars, and then bent down to pray quietly before the *mehrab*.

Afterwards, we walked for miles through the bazaars, past electric tatooing saloons, shops filled with sweetmeats, fruits, giant radishes, slabs of pressed dates and nuts, and dreadful shops where camels' heads lolled out their tongues, death turning the customary disdainful expression to one of langour.

The next morning we bought some fresh eggs from a smiling Bedouin woman outside the hotel, and set off early. We breakfasted on the Mount of Olives, so as to be able to look back at the Old City: swags of bougainvillaea hung like curtains of Tyrian purple over the golden walls, and above it all rose the great shining Dome of the Rock.

K

❊ 14 ❊

The Nabataean City

Amman that day was en fête, and beflagged for the return of the King of the Hashemite Kingdom from a long series of visits abroad.

Amman, Raboth of the Bible and Ptolemy's Philadelphia, today the capital of Jordan, is a little white town clambering up a steep hillside.

We went to enquire at the office of the Antiquities Department about Ahmat Shistewa's proposed invitation to the Jerash Army Day celebrations on May 26th. The officials were kind and helpful but they could not immediately produce a card, for arrangements had to be made first with the Prime Minister's office, so we were asked to return on May 25th when we should be able to collect an official invitation.

I do not know if it were the aftermath of Jerusalem, or a chill caught at Ba'albek, but we both felt rather limp and exhausted that day, so we decided to have a decent meal in the hotel opposite the ruined Roman theatre in the heart of Amman. We left Ark outside the office of the Antiquities Department beside the theatre, and from where we sat on the cool, tree-shaded verandah we could see our homely little van, dwarfed by the tiers of the Roman amphitheatre beyond the hotel gardens of squat palms, bougainvillaeas and pink geraniums. Amman is in every way a mixture of the Biblical, the Hellenistic, the touristic and the modern Jordanian : we sipped iced drinks and watched American tourists arriving, and Muslims saying their noon prayers on the steps of the Roman theatre across the road.

As we left Amman that afternoon people were already lining the streets to welcome their King. We were uncertain which road to take, and enquired of a traffic policemen : 'Petra—please?'

'This gradient—to Kerak!' came the prompt reply, and with a flourish of his baton he indicated the way.

146

It certainly was a *gradient* : Ark surged up it out of Amman and onto the desert road for Medeba and El Kerak.

Later, beyond Medeba, we came to the brink of the great wadi of the 'brook Arnon', so magnificent was it that we decided to settle for the night on its edge—our most awe-inspiring camp since the one under Mount Ararat.

Next day it was hot immediately the sun rose at five a.m., and we looked down again with not a little apprehension at that stupendous gorge, 2,000 feet deep, and at our road twisting its painful way through it up to the flat tableland that stretched warm and brown against an utterly cloudless hot, blue sky. The top was like a great castle wall, and the strata below fell away like some gigantic glacis.

It was an exciting road, comparable in our recent experiences only to the Chalus, but neither so well graded nor so well surfaced. Near the bottom were traces of the old Roman road, marked by some huge milestones. The road was metalled as far as the 'brook', after which the surface was loose, rough and gravelly. Stuart drove : we were both silent, our mouths dry with tension as Ark toiled on, and up and up in bottom most of the time. The width of the gorge at the top is only two miles, but the road is eleven miles long, and it took Ark a breathless thirty-seven minutes to negotiate it. Luckily we met no oncoming vehicles until nearly at the top.

Shortly after we had passed through this wadi, Stuart complained of feeling rather strange and unwell, so he went to sleep in the back while I drove on.

El Kerak, the ancient Kir Moab of the Bible, is a beautiful old village of pale-coloured houses climbing steeply up the hill-side under a fine Crusader castle. Here we had to report at our first militia post of the day. Stuart seemed a little better, but was rather short with me, unlike himself, and presently he again got into the back and slept.

The Bedouin in this area were much darker and wilder-looking than any we had yet seen, the women with their blue-beard tattoos were lean and darkly sunburnt—desert witches in dusty black robes.

Then the road began to drop down into Wadi el Hasa, the River Zared. I drove down without difficulty to the sunbaked valley bottom which was full of pink oleanders, but on the ascent

I grew alarmed, chugging up the narrow rocky road and at each steep corner praying I would not meet another vehicle. At one point, as Ark bounded in bottom gear over a transverse slab of rock at the foot of a particularly sharp incline, maps, books and papers shot out of the roof nets and hit me on the head, I grabbed one of our passports only just in time as it was about to fly out of the window; while my feet were littered in cigarettes, dried plums, apricots and nuts that showered off the dashboard ledge so thickly that I could hardly move the gear lever. But it was not all this that scared me, it was the fact that Stuart could sleep through such a shaking. I began to feel really frightened, and to think that he must be seriously ill. There was no sound from him, although I had yelled as I groped among the plums and nuts and kicked away the cigarettes. But there was nothing I could do at the moment except drive on, I dare not stop for fear of being unable to start again on the gradient. Then, as I neared the top I saw a Bedouin child dashing out of his tent and preparing to hurl a rock at the Ark from a high bank above the road. I changed up into second, Ark gathered speed just in time as the gradient lessened, and the rock fell short.

After another mile or two, well clear of the Bedouin, I stopped to sort myself out, to clear up the debris around my feet, and discover what had happened to Stuart. He awoke, apparently quite himself again and was full of sympathy at my tale of the wadi. But I was still anxious and puzzled, I did not see how he could have been unaware of that road, I thought perhaps he had a touch of the sun. He took some aspirin, and for a while was all right; he then drove on to Tafilia, where the militia were most friendly and insisted on our having cups of tea. But there Stuart again felt ill; after a pause we continued until we came upon a place near Dhana, where the road, skirting along the hillside looks down on a spectacular wadi, leading the eye all the way to the Wadi Araba, the Rift Valley, far below south of the Dead Sea.

The sky was dusky pink near the horizon, then egg-shell blue, giving way to deep cobalt, and the Rift Valley lay below in drowsy, splendid perspective. Here it was not hard to realize the vastness of the Rift—stretching away into Sinai, the Red Sea and to the heart of Africa.

The road became increasingly bad, the surface ruts and rubble; Stuart once more retreated to bed. To make matters worse, in the

late afternoon I took a wrong turning and found myself in Shobak
under the magnificent crumbling pile of yet another Crusader
castle; the villagers were helpful and Stuart awoke but the road
was very narrow and the turning difficult. I began to feel that we
should never find the Spring of Moses* and the village of Elji that
night. At Elji one must leave one's car, and it had been our intention to sleep in the fort there, before riding into Petra in the
morning.

The worsening road wound into a little golden valley that, to
my jaundiced and unhappy eye seemed to be black with Bedouin.
At last, too exhausted to go any further and regardless now of
Bedouin, we stopped after dark, only just off the track, heated
some soup and went to sleep.

The next morning I crawled out over Stuart, and lit the volcano
kettle on the roadside. This and the following one were the only
mornings during the entire journey that I made the early tea. I am
slightly ashamed to admit this, but it was not altogether due to
laziness on my part : the sardine fashion in which we had to sleep
—I lay on the inner side—made it difficult for me to get dressed
and out of the van before Stuart was up—a good excuse no doubt,
for I managed it well enough that morning. I was still extremely
worried about him. Petra was now so near : it could not be more
than a few miles away, and yet I feared that the only sensible
thing to do would be to go back. However, Stuart drank his tea,
and when he was fully awake he announced that he felt a little
better, and refused point blank to return.

So we rattled and bounced on along the track; it was the
shortest day's run of the trek—for Ain Musa lay five miles ahead.

From Calcutta to this tiny place in the wilderness of south
Jordan the Ark had travelled 7,206 miles. Ain Musa the Spring
of Moses, is mentioned in the Koran as the place where Moses
cleft the rock. The stream which flows from it is the one that
formerly watered the ancient Nabataean capital of Petra; it rises
from a narrow gulley among fig trees and olives. As we drove up
to it so wanly that early morning, some armed Arabs were drawing water, their horses standing tethered by. There was no sign
of Petra beyond the pale limestone hills of Edom in the south-west,
in which I supposed it lay. Small wonder that fabulous Petra and
indeed 'all knowledge of the site of this unique city was lost to the

* Ain Musa.

Western world from the time of the Crusades, about A.D. 1200 until 1812, when a young Anglo-Swiss explorer named Burckhardt rediscovered it.'*

We went on directly to the fortress outpost at Elji where ponies for the ride into Petra are obtained. The fort is manned by men of the militia, in khaki breeches and red *khaffiyeh*, but there was one young English-speaking man in smart drill uniform and the spiked and aproned helmet of the civil police, posted there specially to assist tourists, and to him, after a while, I was able to explain how ill Stuart was—as indeed I think they could all see for themselves. When they had fully grasped the situation they allowed us to take Ark inside the fort, where we decided to rest until Stuart should feel strong enough for Petra. We parked in a scrap of shade under a little tree in the central courtyard, and Stuart—with his usual determination—set about the job of getting well.

I shall always be grateful to our Australian doctor and friend in Malaya, who had equipped us with a supply of medicines for various contingencies. She had said that should we ever be really in a fix cremasuxidine plus terramycine would be most likely to do the trick, so I now started to give Stuart both at regular intervals. Throughout that day, he dozed and rested, waking only for his medicine, and for cups of clear tea, or of consommé soup.

After mid-day it grew intensely hot and the flies buzzed under that little tree. The soldiers sat in the shade by Ark, drinking tea and gambling, and sometimes the young policeman came inside to talk with me, or to bring kettles of hot mint tea made by his wife. Outside the fort, the cars of a few tourists from Amman or Ma'an were waiting in the shade, their drivers asleep, among the wretched caravans of dejected fly-haunted ponies.

I worked hard that day, trying not to worry unduly. I had great faith in Stuart's ability to overcome illness, he was no longer scratchy, and it seemed that whatever had attacked him the worst was over, but he was very weak. My own insides were behaving in a slightly peculiar manner, but luckily I did not feel at all ill.

We were introduced to our guide, Abu Ali, an elderly Bedouin, said to be the most reliable in Petra though he looked a lazy, happy-go-lucky old reprobate. He was to wait and see how we were in the morning. These so-called guides are virtually thrust

* *The Antiquities of Jordan,* G. Lankester Harding.

upon one by the Government, for foreigners are not permitted into Petra unaccompanied.

'O thou that dwellest in the clefts of the rock, that holdest the height of the hill : though thou shouldest make thy nest as high as the eagle, I will bring thee from thence, saith the Lord.' So prophesied Jeremiah for the inhabitants of Sela in the wilderness—the name Petra corresponds to the Hebrew *Sela,* a rock which in Arabic means cleft of a rock. 'Also Edom shall be a desolation : and everyone that goeth by it shall be astonished. . . .'*

Now we seemed to be living in the Old Testament, every day it was becoming more alive with a wealth of new meaning and reality in that wonderful wilderness. Edom is the hill land that guards Petra to the north-east, and the gloomy prophecies of Jeremiah have come to pass only too well because—so the Old Testament preaches—of the wrath of God upon those who made sacrifices to the false gods on the High Places.

The people who found this almost impregnable site and made it their own were the Nabataeans, originally a wandering Arabic tribe who settled in Petra, and who grew rich by raiding caravans passing on the inland route from Egypt to Syria, and who later, under good kings of their own, settled down, levied proper taxes on these caravans and traded far and wide themselves. Their sway at one time extended as far north as Damascus. They occupied Petra from the fifth century B.C. until the fifth century A.D. Egyptian influences are clear in their city and—it has been suggested—even Indian ones, and later after Antigonus captured Petra in 312 B.C., the Roman influence was strong. But most strange of all is a kind of foretaste of an architecture of quite another style not then yet born, of which I shall write later.

After another good night's sleep Stuart, although feeling rather weak, insisted that he was now well enough to enter Petra. We packed a donkey bag, sketch bag, and rucksack, and leaving the Ark inside the fort with the tea-drinking militia, we called Abu Ali, and amid much shouting and fuss mounted our decrepit ponies and began tottering down through the steep village of Elji towards the pale sandstone hills that hid Petra from sight.

I was, of course, immensely excited to be entering Petra at last, but I was still concerned about Stuart, for despite the warmth of the sun he was wearing two or three layers of clothing and I

* Jeremiah, 49. 16-17.

noticed that he seemed to sway a little on his aged mount. Our
ponies were led by boys, and there were no reins, but after a
while we made the bridle ropes into reins by knotting them together, both of us disliking the slipshod indignity of being led. As
we progressed noisily through the village Abu Ali was busy rushing about in the distance on the mountainside, calling out to some
unseen friends. A small donkey carrying our gear and cameras led
our rather disorderly little cavalcade down the hot ravine. As we
went, a string of camels crossed the valley and began swiftly
mounting up the side of the hill on our left, and weird shouts
echoed off the rocks—old Abu Ali was engaged in argument with
the camel drivers.

Among this jumble of pale sandstone rocks and cliffs and a few
tombs ahead there was still no sign of the hidden entrance to Petra.
But I knew that soon we must come to El Siq—the high narrow
cleft that for so long made Petra invincible, even to the Romans,
and that through later centuries hid it from the world.

Near the entrance to the Siq is a porticoed hewn-out chamber—
the 'Roman kastam Betra'* as Abu Ali called it, in other words the
place where the caravan taxes were levied—and also a shallow
low-roofed Nabataean tomb with a bas relief of donkey and rider,
and two curling snakes. But this was not shown to us until our
return, by which time we had become good friends with Abu Ali.

Then the soft wind that in the next few days came to be so much
a part of Petra, began sighing as the rock walls narrowed about us
and we entered El Siq.

This wind of Petra sounds like the waves of the sea, sighing
among caves, and hollow places, tombs, high niches, sconces and
windows, portals and balustrades, and among little fir trees, red
oleanders and reeds. This was the wind that for thousands of years
has helped to chisel the amazing shapes of Petra's soft sandstone,
so that today it is difficult to tell which was made by man and
which by nature in all the profusion of carving.

The walls of the Siq grew higher and higher above our heads,
and we stopped frequently—to stare and to film.

It was more than awe-inspiring, it was lonely, fantastic and
beautiful—and—all ours—for there were no other tourists. There
was only the sound of that sighing wind, the dry stones rattling and
the noise of our ponies' hooves echoing under the overhanging

---

* Petra's Roman Customs.

cliffs. Sometimes our Arabs called out to each other, their voices ringing and echoing off the massive stone walls. But we ourselves, as we wound deeper into the heart of this vast cleft rock, grew silent and more amazed.

This mysterious elusive exhilarating Petra is unique. Its greatest treasure — El Khazneh — which I knew was lying in wait, as it has done for centuries to startle the traveller with its incredible rosy beauty, must now be close, for the walls of the Siq began to change colour. There was rose-red flushed with tan and rust among the plum-blue and ochre.

I had seen many photographs of El Khazneh, and I expected perhaps to be disappointed. But as the rock walls suddenly twisted and parted to reveal a little of its sunlit warmth and splendour framed in their dark curving stone, we stopped, as all travellers must, dazzled by its glory; and then moved slowly on until the full beauty of the high façade came into sight.

El Khazneh is the hollow empty tomb of a Nabataean king carved in living rock, out of the sheer dark face of the hill itself. *This,* of course, is the wonder of Petra, that all its amazing artefacts are carved, not built.

Its height, depth and colouring were startling in the hot, early morning sunlight; the ravine is so narrow that the tomb's façade is in the sunlight for only a short time each day — and this was the hour. Above a mass of deep pink oleanders in full flower it stood silent, exquisite as if smiling out of the dark cliff. The Arabs called it El Khazneh Phaaron — the Pharaoh's Treasury, because they believed that the urn on the top, above the little central circular pavilion or tholus, enshrined a hoard of gold, and for years it was their habit to fire at this urn as if in the hope of cracking a giant jack-pot.

El Khazneh is of a later period than much of Petra, probably of the second century A.D., and like El Deir — that is hidden high in the hills — it belongs to that extraordinary forecast in architectural evolution as if by some magic a touch of seventeenth century Baroque had flowered suddenly and prematurely in Roman Petra.

Its façade seems enormously high. Some say it is eighty or ninety feet, others only sixty-five, but whatever its height, it has a whispering flower-coloured mellow beauty soaring from the oleanders at its foot. It seems as if it were animated, and is well aware of the

shock of delight it gives to each traveller emerging from the dark
and narrow Siq.

Now we had to ride on. We had dawdled so long that it was
late and the pony boys had to return to school. So Abu Ali sent
them back, they dived into the darkness of the Siq and disappeared. We turned to the right, down the Wadi Musa where it
begins to widen, and rode on in silence still dazzled by the Khazneh, and now by the sight of the innumerable tombs and rock
dwellings in the hills opening out all around. Where the valley
widened, the Romans had cut a theatre from one great slab of
rock, slicing through much older Nabataean tombs so that they
give the effect of galleries above the seats.

Then the valley spreads wide into a great amphitheatre of hills
—El Habis ahead, with Umm el Biyara, Mother of Cisterns, and
Jebel el Deir, Mountain of the Monastery, hemming in the way.
It is thought to be from the sheer heights of Umm el Biyara that
ten thousand unfortunate Edomite captives were flung down after
being defeated in battle by Amaziah king of Judah. According
to Lankester Hardinge the mountain people the Horites (of Mount
Hor) were the first inhabitants of Petra, they were driven out by
the Edomites, who in their turn were overcome by the Nabataeans,
who were themselves eventually conquered but not driven out by
the Romans.

The Roman city lies in ruins in the heart of the valley close
under El Habis; the Nabataean rock dwellings are empty and
silent except for a handful of Bedouin who eke out a meagre
existence there. For, as Jeremiah prophesied, the place has become
a desolation—today the water is still failing, and the once great
city lies quiet and parched under the fiery hot bowl of the sky.

After another twenty minutes we were on the remains of the
Roman road that follows beside the dry river bed—now brimming
with dark flowering oleanders—we rode under the broken triumphal arch, and past the earthquake-shattered Roman temple to the
little 'camp'. The 'camp' is a small stone building shaded by
eucalyptus trees, well disguised, and hidden between the ruined
temple and the hill of El Habis.

We spent four and a half crowded and intensely happy days in
Petra, walking, exploring, filming, painting. But one could spend
months in there and still not know the half of it; each hour

brought a fresh vision, and new queries, and left countless mysteries unexplained.

We acquired the services of a donkey man, 'donk man', as Abu Ali called him, Jumar, a sprightly young ex-soldier who turned actor for our filming, chasing his curly black-haired goats about the hillside, a small bounding figure in black aba and flowing white *khaffiyeh*, dwarfed by the huge façades of the tombs.

Petra is not all 'rose-red' as Burgon described it, but it is many coloured, and the Nabataeans, by carving into solid rock revealed the range of natural colours that would otherwise have been hidden in the heart of the stone. The interiors of the tombs are unadorned except by these natural swirling patterns in the smoothly chiselled living rock, patterns exactly like those of watered silks— blue, tan, cream and terracotta, and infinitely more lovely than any ordinary man-made mosaic.

Was the Nabataean's really a cult of the dead? If so, why did the classical commentator Strabo, in the first century B.C. record that they had no care for their corpses and merely cast them down beside their privies?* In many ways Petra remains mysterious.

One day I was sitting up by the north-east face, painting, with old Abu Ali half-asleep on guard at my elbow when a witch-like woman appeared, small and thin in torn black robes and dwarfed by the great background of coloured stone. She might have come out of 'Macbeth', and I almost expected to see her float up from the shadows into the hot still air above. She kept her distance, but voices screamed out in the high Arab call; another woman appeared, a baby in her arms, and a heated discussion ensued between Abu Ali close at my side and the two Bedouin witches.

The baby wailed and was put to the breast, and for a time there was silence, until suddenly 'el Donk' began braying his fierce, harsh sunset call down by El Habis, and then all at once more Arab voices began echoing around the great silent hills. A good-looking man, armed with a rifle, joined the two tattered women and came to greet me and to inspect my work.

I discovered then that the little woman with the baby was Jumar's wife. The contrast of most Bedouin women with their menfolk was marked: the men clean and better dressed, the women pathetically tattered and grimed. They are a very dark-

---

* Lankaster Hardinge comments amusingly on this in his *The Antiquities of Jordan*.

faced people almost as black as Tamils—though some of it may be dirt—indeed the feet and ankles of the children have a leathery look with the dust and dirt. Many Bedouin have a slight caste in one eye—as Jumar had—a result, so I was told, of malnutrition in childhood. Indeed their state of poverty was very pitiful, but despite it, most of them, the men especially, have a wonderful naïve cheerfulness, a gaiety of manner and a spontaneity that was touching and appealing.

One afternoon Jumar sat for me near the Roman theatre in the shade of the valley. He posed well, unselfconsciously, and when he saw the result, he was so pleased that he doubled up, yelled with delight, wrung my hand warmly and called out loudly for Abu Ali who was, of course, dozing somewhere in the shade nearby. After the polite, careful way Malay men have with European women, I found these Arabs very hail-fellow-well-met with their slaps on the back and hearty handshakes. But Stuart and I both took to Jumar immensely.

One morning we went to El Thogra the so-called Snake Monument, with Abu Ali, Jumar and el Donk. It is in a strange valley dominated by Umm el Biyaria and the sharp cone of Mount Hor. On either side near the Thogra itself stand two huge square-topped stones that from the distance look like built-up guard rooms but which on approach seem to melt into the landscape, and are like the rest of Petra—carved, not built.

Bearing our gear, el Donk leapt about lightly on his little ballet dancer feet and later rested in the shade with Abu Ali, while Jumar, Stuart and I went about exploring. On most of these excursions Abu Ali would wander off at some point, his powerful voice ringing out down the valleys and among the tombs until he met a Bedouin or two—they seemed to spring up from nowhere like dark sprites—and from them he would buy goat's milk for his supper. In one of the caves near the camp there was a tiny shop where he could buy sugar and a few other things; we were expected to keep him supplied with cigarettes. He always made a great show of gallantly offering me el Donk to ride, while obviously praying that I would not. Generally I did not, but on the few occasions when I did—mainly to ease el Donk from his much greater load—I discovered the reason why donkey riders from Iran to Greece swing their legs. It is the only way to stay on these energetic animals!

With the two men we climbed up also to El Deir, and to the High Place, Jumar carrying most of the gear, for even el Donk could not manage those stairways and sheer rock faces.

One of the chief gods of the Nabataeans was Dushara (Jehovah or Adonai) and he was represented by small, standing, blocks of stone or obelisks, most of which have vanished. But in many places, in the corners of such staircases as the beautiful weather-worn rose-flushed one at El Deir, there are little hollowed-out shrines which must once have housed the 'god stones', which were perhaps much the same as the 'god boxes' of ancient Byblos.

El Deir, the so-called monastery, is an enormous tomb, bigger than El Khazneh and yet quite concealed on its high hill top* It was not until I watched Stuart and Jumar (Abu, of course, was sleeping in the shade somewhere) walk across the courtyard to the gaping black portal, that I realized the tomb's size—it is over 140 feet high. I watched their tiny figures clamber up to the threshold like Lilliputians and disappear inside.

From the top of the col beyond El Deir, there was a stupendous view, over a vertical mile down to Wadi Araba towards the Gulf of Akaba, and the mountains of Sinai in the distance. I gazed down with an intense renewal of my old longing to see those places; but this was as far south as we could go. Shortage of time and funds now put Akaba and Sinai beyond our reach.

From El Deir, we could see Mount Hor, and when we pointed it out to Abu Ali he appeared not to have realized that it was visible from the col. Its tiny white mosque or shrine, said to be the tomb of Aaron,* was a small dot near the summit. He exclaimed, his voice dropping as if with awe : 'Ah ! — Musjid Nabi Haroun !' and gesturing reverently towards the distant height, he bowed and touched his hand to eyes, lips and heart.

On the way down, we discovered one or two little cisterns that were still full of water, 'special' water which Jumar eagerly invited us to drink—perhaps the shrines of Allat, the Nabataeans' god of clear water.

In the wadi below Jebel el Deir there are shapes, a hint of tombs half-cut in the sheer angled rock walls—or carved by

* It reminds one irresistibly of London Baroque carved massively out of the crown of the wild mountain top. . . .

* 'And Aaron was an hundred and twenty-three years old when he died in Mount Hor.' Numbers 33.39.

nature, we could not tell—and here too are many rock dwellings with wild 'red-hot pokers' and little senna trees flowering at their doorsteps. Some of these dwellings are three-storeyed. It was not hard to imagine the old wives of Petra calling out to each other across the stream, while they worked at their household chores and came and went to market, especially at one narrow corner where the dwellings were close face to face. Yet now all was quiet, hot and still—a dead place—we met only one aged crone, and later a little tired-faced boy washing himself in the trickle that runs among the oleanders, while his silky black goats, satyr-like, drank among the red flowers stirring up the honeyed almond scent. Above the deep wadi and above the high barren peaks of El Deir, Pharaoh's chickens soared white in the blue.

On the last afternoon we climbed to the High Place of Sacrifice. It overlooks the wadi below, and the large tombs of the north-east face, so that one can clearly see how their tall majestic façades were carved from the strata.

The words of the Bible—'the high places'—now evoke for me a wonderful image, a smooth splendid elevation of stone, lifted to the hot blue sky high above a city—a natural altar raised to heaven—it is scarcely surprising that such Places were used for worship.

When we arrived at last on this splendid height, Jumar ran gaily onto the sacrificial stone and flung himself down on its central slab. At once old Abu Ali joined in the spirit of the game; bounding forward he drew his silver Arab dagger and posed dramatically, ready to slit young Jumar's throat.

I asked them to repeat the performance so that we might film it. When it was done, the 'sacrifice' sat up laughing heartily, but suddenly a shadow passed across Abu's face and he said : 'If people see that in London—they think Arabs are *bad* men . . .?'

I recalled what Abdul Rahman had said, and told him that it wouldn't be so, for I'd finally filmed the 'sacrifice' alive and laughing. Reassured he sank down happily on the steps of the little altar, and drank neatly from one of our bottles, pouring the water down his throat as was his habit, skilfully, without touching his lips to the aperture.

But Jumar went running about the shorn-off height, his white and black *khaffiyeh* flying out behind him, luminous against the sun-hazed, heat-filled hills far below—the burning hills of Edom.

The next day it was time to leave, and to say goodbye to those two cheerful men who had shown a warmth of good humour towards us both. Bedouin are highly emotional people : the parting was quite moving, and I was amazed to see that tears stood in Jumar's eyes as we shook hands before riding away out of Petra, the 'strong city'.

✷ 15 ✷

Whitsun with Adonis;
and East again to Palmyra

The drive back from Petra was very different from the outward
one. Now perfectly fit again, Stuart was anxious to see all that he
had missed. We were both intensely happy, refreshed and exhilarated by Petra, and able now to laugh at my fears, and at the difficulties of the road.

At El Kerak we ceremoniously drank Arab coffee with the
Chief of Police, and were shown over the Crusader castle by an
elegant young policeman, who later helped, in a most natural way,
to shop for melons, wine and apricots, and to fend off the singu-
larly cheeky children of that steep little town, all as if it were but
a part of his routine.

At the Tafilia militia post we were welcomed as old friends,
entertained to tea again under the walnut trees and—because I
had done some drawing there previously—the fat sergeant in com-
mand insisted on posing while one of his men played Arab music
on the *rebana*. In the course of this session we discovered many
Arab words in common with Malay.

With all these stops and an abortive search for an elusive
Nabataean monument, we did not make much progress that day,
so at sunset we camped again above the splendid Wadi Mujib, of
the brook Arnon.

In Amman, the next morning we collected the official
invitation to the Jerash celebrations from the Prime Minister's
office—the same modern building which was blown up in an
attempt to assassinate King Hussein a few months later.

In Jerash again we had a new camping place. We watched the
King arrive by helicopter for a fleeting visit during the day, and we
listened to the clear falsetto Arab voices practising their songs in
the pomegranate grove above.

In the evening we walked up the hillside, stepping over little clear rivulets that irrigated small tilled plots, to the forum, to await the second arrival of King Hussein, and the start of the show.

The floodlit forum looked magnificent; behind it long tables now laden with food stretched half the length of the colonnaded street. Under the glowing Ionic pillars, soldiers were serving Bedouin coffee from gleaming brass coffee pots nestling in hot charcoal embers. There was a gentle skirl of the bagpipes mingling with the urgent African rhythm of the coffee pounder's pestle and on the hillsides above, the rose-red colour of the soldiers' *khaffiyehs* sang out behind the slender lighted columns.

When the young King arrived, the people in the crowded forum got to their feet, and the soldiers on the hillside above leapt up yelling—'*Qwayis! Qyawis!*', flinging their red *khaffiyehs* in the air.

The show was a lengthy business, and one could have done with something stronger than coffee. There were Arab, Circassian, Cossack and Bedouin songs and dances. I liked best the eerie Bedouin dances with their persistent, haunting, monotonous rhythm, and high falsetto voices; and rows of male dancers in white robes who bounced, clapped and shrilled like a lot of lusty angels to the music of a lively African flutist. These men—holding hands and looking like angels without wings—were the toughest of soldiers, who come from El Kerak, a place that has some reputation for ferocity.

When it was over the young King went to wash his hands at a special basin half-concealed in leaves at the entrance to the colonnaded street, the vast audience followed him and dinner was served. He stood at the head of the table, in front of an enormous, galantine of meat formed in the shape of a kneeling camel. He is a small handsome smiling young man, but I noticed that he spoke only very little, as if the burden of kingship were heavy.

The following morning we took a protracted farewell of our Jerash friends over cups of tea, and eventually set off. But we got no further than the village post office. There, in an attempt to buy a few stamps, we were entertained by the post-master, a volatile, irritable, enchantingly theatrical man, friend of Ahmat Shistewa. Over coffee, brought from his house by one of his five little daughters, he recounted his life story; enlarged at some length on his own habit of 'playing politics'—the reason for his present post-

L

ing; talked about the British Army in which he had served for several years; of English dialects and family planning. All this in intervals of roaring belligerently down the telephone; sweating profusely and mopping his brow on a red ink-stained rag; raging at a junior official; storming, and smiling and, in a kind of despairing way, looking around for those stamps for our letters. At last he found them, beamed at us, and continued with his story.

'Now politics finish!' he bellowed. '*Children* finish too—five is enough!'

The telephone bell rang: it was Ahmat Shistewa. He must have guessed that something of this sort would happen to us in the Post Office; we had been there forty-five minutes already, and now he had rung to say 'goodbye' once more.

The postmaster took the hint: at last our letters were stamped and marked with tremendous gusto and military precision, and we rose to go. But he was still talking fifteen minutes later as we walked into the sunshine, and began drifting gently towards Ark.

We had no desire to leave Jordan, a friendly, kindly country, and its lovable, charming people. We were looking forward to seeing Abdul Rahman again before crossing back into Syria, but we made a stupid mistake. That evening we visited the ruined black basalt city and castle of Umm el Jamal off the Baghdad road on a dark desert plain, and on the following morning, having taken this different route we overshot the turning to Abdul Rahman's village and found ourselves all too soon at the Syrian frontier. It was a disappointment, but by then it was too far and too late to turn back.

Umm el Jamal, 'the Mother of Camels', too had been something of a disappointment, all drab lava stone rising from the equally black desert. Its only magnificence was in our soldier escort who wore red and gold on a long flowing uniform, and the immensity of its slab-like basalt doors that gave some idea of the power once vested in this strange deserted city.

Our camp that night, not from the eerie pile of its ruins, was the first entirely visitorless one of our whole journey. Turning on the radio in this empty loneliness, we learnt of the *coup* in Turkey, and wondered again what we should do if things became too difficult for travel there. It would be a nuisance if we were forced to ship from Beirut to Athens.

We visited Damascus next day only briefly, the *souks* were entertaining, the mosque beautiful, the cooked food shops were good, and we bought some delectable stuffed aubergines, and other hot delicacies for our lunch.

On the way from Damascus to Homs there are traces of the Roman road, especially interesting where it had been carved from solid rock and cut with inscriptions. But we were none too pleased to be in Syria again, with its bad drivers, and atmosphere so different from that of Jordan.

There were great flocks of black and white cranes flying from Homs Lake, and once a vulture swooped low to snatch a snake off the road. Somewhere in the uplands on the way to Homs we pulled off at the roadside for a drink of water, and rather to our surprise, for we took him to be a Syrian, a lorry driver drew up to offer help. We gave him a drink and offered him a 'Petra' cigarette, when he saw the pink carton, he said at once that he himself was from Jordan and his face lit up with a wide smile. 'Wait—I go get you a bahnahnah!'

He dashed back to his lorry and returned with not just a single banana, but two enormous bunches of them.

That night, we could not reach Krak des Chevaliers, our next point of call, so we camped in the empty uplands above Homs Lake. The wind was too high to cook anything except hot water in the volcano kettle.

Krak was one of the places we had long planned to see, about which much has been written. T. E. Lawrence said that it is 'perhaps the best preserved and most wholly admirable castle in the world.'

As we approached it on the following morning in the high wind, on a ghastly steep and stony road, a large retinue of Syrian Government cars swept past. The castle towered above us, in a wild wind-torn sky; there were peasants at work in the fields— golden grain against a stormy background, a fit setting for the grey Norman stronghold. It was held for 150 years without a break and was surrendered in the end only through enemy trickery. Part of its walls are eighty feet thick and it is so impressive that it was known to the Muslims as 'the Mountain'.

We continued up the alarmingly steep gradient through a village of screamingly pestiferous children. But once safely inside the castle we had the whole magnificent place almost to ourselves —the official party having vanished, apparently onto the tableland beyond. A young custodian showed us round, assisted by two small boys and a pathetic mentally deficient child, who as a baby had fallen from one of the high walls and never fully recovered.

Despite this oddly assorted little entourage of young Syrians one felt it was not very long ago since the Crusader cavalcades had clattered up the long corridors in the fortress.

That evening we crossed back again into the Lebanon. The strong wind was still blowing madly from the west, in the fields sweet-corn tossed wildly, its long ribbony green leaves waving towards the east. At the frontier we had a remarkably pleasant welcome : a bored young official rose up from a bed behind his desk, asked if we were tired, and produced successively—Turkish coffee, pistachio nuts, and Scotch whisky.

Our camp was by the sea that night, in a P.W.D. gravel pit, to which friendly donkey boys came and went on their work but none bothered us.

Despite the wind I plucked up the courage to bathe, and the next morning we drove on towards Byblos which seemed more enchanting each time one saw it afresh—and so down into Beirut, where we spent the next few day again in its luxurious atmosphere.

One sunny day Lionel* took us to see the Ottoman Empire palace of Emir Bechir at Beit ed Din. A sumptuous place with fountains, and elegant courtyards, a harem behind the cypress trees, a hamman formed like a maze, and fascinating little reception rooms in one of which water ran down over a mother-of-pearl inlaid wall panel.

With Ba* another day we lunched high in the hills above Beirut at the holiday house of some friends. The view was glorious and the Lebanese food delicious, but I mostly remember that house for the decision made there. At lunch Stuart changed his mind about Palmyra, and agreed—as I had so long hoped—to go there after all : it would be our last look at the desert, our last diversion eastwards.

Lebanon's coastline is only one hundred and thirty miles long, and when we had driven south to Tyre and Sidon we had seen the length of it. The high wind was still blowing madly, and in dusty ruined Tyre it was hard to imagine ancient splendours, but Sidon was more impressive. We explored what is left of the castle, so

---

* Ba and Lionel Gorra—Stuart's niece and her husband with whom we stayed each time in Beirut.

dramatically set out into the dark sea, broken and lively that day with wild white horses . . .

The day we left Beirut was Whit Saturday; we lunched with Ba and Lionel at a little restaurant in Rue Bliss, and they sent us off armed with two bottles of Ksara wine and a 'rosted' chicken—this time minus the garlic—for supper in the hills. We were now heading for Al Afka, the Holy Source of the Adonis.

At our favourite little Italian café in Byblos the road turns sharp right; very steep and narrow, twisting and climbing into the mountains above. We had no idea where we might sleep for the night, nor where it might be possible to draw off the road. Lionel had been unable to recall any space, although he had thought that it might be just possible at Ain Afka itself where the Adonis gushes out of the mountain.

But shortly before sunset we came to a deep-set, grassy sward, obviously used as a stone dump by road-workers; so once again it was the P.W.D. who solved the question—and it was an ideal place. At 3,500 feet the air was very cold, but the place was beautiful, the well of granite and scrub around darkly cupping the stars and a bright half moon above. It was so cold that I wondered if it was passion alone that kept the naked Adonis and his beautiful Astarte warm up here in the mountains of their legend.

It was still very early when we arrived next morning at Al Afka, the Holy Source. First we explored the deep grotto of the Astarte and Adonis legend, from which the river once poured forth—it has now changed its course to a slightly lower level in the mountain. I would have liked to have seen its waters turn red as they do once a year owing to iron ore deposits, but as if symbolically with the blood of the 'lord'—Adonis; the word comes from the Semitic Adon—lord, and is one and the same with the Syrian Thammuz and with countless other lords.

> 'Thammuz came next behind
> Whose annual wound in Lebanon allur'd
> The Syrian damnsels to lament his fate
> In amorous ditties all a summer's day,
> While smooth Adonis from his native rock
> Ran purple to the sea.'*

* Milton's *Paradise Lost*.

Here in Adonis' myth are all the symbols of the course of the
seasons, fertility and death, spring and renewed life, and too the
origin of Christian Easter gardens, deriving from the same pagan
thought.

There was a twitter of swallows above the roar of the falls; wild
valerian and red poppies grew beside the goat paths, but it was
cold and sunless in the shadow of the great cliffs, and we soon went
down to the ruins of the temple below—the temple in which the
rites of sacred prostitution took place; rituals that deteriorated
into the licentiousness which so offended Constantine.

Destroyed by him, the temple is now little more than a jumbled
mound of grass-covered stone, the Assuan granite brought by the
Romans from Egypt. But below, on one of its walls there is a small
shrine sheltered by an ancient fig tree, and here I saw white votive
rags hung there by today's devotees of the cult that still lingers,
though in a different form—barren women who pray to the 'Lady
of the Place' for a fertile womb.

As I sat warming myself in the sunshine, a tall handsome young
Arab in a navy blue jacket, *khaffiyeh* and baggy Turkish-style
trousers appeared above the shrine with two young boys, they
watched him creep into the dark little grotto in the wall. I also
watched from my sunny rock. Inside he lit five candles; he remained there for some time as if in prayer, and had removed his
khaffiyeh and the skull cap under it; for an Arab to do so struck
me as being strange. I was puzzled about this, and when he and
the boys had gone away I climbed up to the shrine myself to look
in. I do not know what I had expected to see, but certainly not
this: his candles were burning before faded colour prints of the
Virgin and Child—Sitt Mariam, the Lady Mary, or Sitt el
Matrah, the Lady of the Place—once the goddess Astarte. A
strange mixture of pagan, Christian and Islamic!

After a while Stuart and I went down to a rough terrace café
roofed over with branches that stood close to the falls of Adonis.
The young Arab in the dark jacket was sitting here now with his
friends, and when he saw us he went to the edge of roaring Adonis,
and blew loudly upon a whistle to summon the café proprietress
from her work in a potato patch far below. She toiled up to take
our orders, and smilingly fetched icy cold water in a green glass
flagon and beer cold from a pool on the lip of the falls.

I was so cold that although it was only eight o'clock in the morning Stuart gave me raki to warm me, and as we sat nibbling pistachio nuts and sipping our drinks, I began to draw.

Despite language difficulties we made friends with some of the country Arabs who joined us then, and one of them seeing how chilled I was in the icy shadow of the mountain presently taught me an Arab dance which was more warming than the raki.

After a while we said goodbye, left the Source, and when we had come down out of the mountains we spent the rest of the morning in golden Byblos. We lunched once more at the little Italian café on the corner, and then drifted on northwards along the coast. Election-conscious Lebanon was very much on holiday, and at the roadside men were selling the first of the small green figs and fresh almonds green in their shells.

We slept by the sea that night and the next morning entered Syria again—Palmyra, the half-way oasis was our destination that day. Coming down towards Homs again we saw the blue of the Great Syrian Desert far below stretching away beyond the 'ports of the desert' like a sea, towards Dura Europa on the distant Euphrates.

Under King Odenathus, and later under that romantic and dashing woman—his widow, Queen Zenobia, Palmyra* rendered service to Rome in battle against the Persians. It was under Zenobia that Palmyra reached the zenith of its fame, but it was her ambition that finally caused her ruin and the fall of Palmyra.

The Palmyrenes must have been a fascinating people : they spoke Aramaic, the language of Christ, but the upper classes also spoke Greek and Latin and they had adopted a kind of desert Graeco-Roman culture that was distinctly individual.

The road—if it can be so called—to Palmyra is one hundred miles long running beside the new pipe-line. It is in fact a stone track; around it, like sound waves, run six, eight and sometimes even more tracks diverging from but roughly following, the central stone one. It appears that no one ever uses the main track except perhaps after heavy rain. We weaved, bumped and wound our way slowly over those hot one hundred miles of desert. It was lonely but with nothing approaching the remoteness of Baluchistan.

We had two punctures that day and it seemed as if we should

* The Tadmor of the Bible, Tudmur in modern Arabic.

never reach Palmyra. By evening we were still driving east, the
moon, now nearing the full again, stood bone white in the hot sky
ahead. The desert seemed to slope eternally down, always beyond
to the Euphrates, in strange shapes of pinkish hills and rocks, with
a glitter—a hint of electric blue, like dark livid fire—the lone level
sands stretching far away, above the warm-coloured middle distance.

Before Ark's laborious progress a covey or two of sand grouse
rose on greyish wings. Now hills began to close in on either side
of the vast shallow valley through which we were travelling. An
acute blue-shadowed escarpment stood to the north, and then a
castle appeared, apricot pink, light against that absymal blue
beyond—the blue that looks like the sea. Was this at last the gateway that hid Palmyra?

Suddenly a mob of small but ferocious children materialized,
running hard with uplifted sticks, and yelling fiercely for baksheesh. Their huts, as we could see now, lay far away at one side
of the valley.

Then at last we were through the valley and quite alone; and
Palmyra's fabulous ruins in their dark oasis lay below; golden in
the sunset. In the rapidly dying light the huge temple of Ba'al, the
long colonnaded street, the houses and temples glowed apricot-
coloured in their dark setting of date palms, isolated in the vast
wilderness all around.

We stood on the shoulder of the hill, gazing down in silence for
a few short moments as the great moon brightened and the colours
faded from the ruins, and from the rose-red and blue of the wilderness that stretched from the oasis, tilting down, and away towards
the still far distant Euphrates—'to the uttermost sea'.

That alone was worth the appalling drive. We walked back to
Ark where we had left her on the hillside and began to settle in for
the night : we would drop down to the oasis early in the morning.

To this wonderful lonely spot tonight Ark had travelled 8,200
miles from Calcutta. We settled down in the moonlit desert, and
had no visitors at all until eight o'clock next morning when a herd
of camels strode slowly, majestically up over the rim of the hill.
Their two young Bedouin attendants were content with a cigarette
each.

Not so the children and youths of Palmyra itself. In some parts
of this gorgeous relic of a fantastic empire one is so much at the

mercy of a pestering, begging and near assaulting mob of nomad offspring now settled in the oasis, that to endeavour to paint there was to endure a mild form of torture. One of the favourite tricks of these boys was to cause their donkeys to bray just as one was putting on a delicate touch, and the song of a Middle Eastern donkey is like the bellowing of a giant dying slowly and in agony.

How Stuart endured all this alongside me I do not know, but he patiently kept me company while I worked, and he even managed to crack jokes with the importunate brats. A running fire of commentary was kept up by both sides—in English, French, Arabic and even Malay, punctuated by an occasional howl from me begging for mercy. Once or twice Stuart leapt out of the car, and made them run for cards or for sweets to give me a moment's respite. When the bedlam was at its worst, Stuart sternly rebuked one boy, commanding him to—'Go Damas!' Perhaps by chance he had hit on some kind of effective local curse, for, to my amazement, the boy took to his heels and fled. But not so the rest, and I do not know which was the worse—their laughter, or their constant whining, jostling, and tapping for baksheesh, or the ghastly braying of their beautiful white donkeys.

Their favourite haunt was beside the Triumphal Arch at the end of the long colonnaded street, and I wondered how the indomitable Lady Hester Stanhope would have dealt with them if only she could have been resurrected. Every time I looked at that arch framing as it does the ruined Turkish castle on the hill top to the west, I thought of her and could picture the triumphant entry she made into Palmyra against all official advice in 1813, when in full Bedouin dress she was crowned Queen of the East by a beautiful Arab dancing girl lowered from the arch itself. Imagination peopled the colonnaded street with Bedouin dancing girls, standing on every one of those votive brackets with which the Palmyrenes in their excessive love of adornment had seen fit to mar the line of each slender column.

But it would take more than the baksheesh boys to spoil Palmyra; with its traditions of the energetic and brave Zenobia; and its great temple to Ba'al,* where the inner shrine so often

* Ba'al was the name of male deities of the Phoenicians and of the Canaanites worshipped on the High Places. Later the name applied only to the Lord of Fertility and of the Sun in whom all the other deities were merged—from which as the latter day 'false god' of the Hebrews the word Beelzebub (Baal Zebub—originally Lord of the Flies) has also derived.

ran with sacrificial blood; and too, perhaps even more than anything in the city, the strange and hauntingly wonderful valley of tombs beyond.

But before I could paint, or we could visit the temple, or do anything else, Ark's tyre had to be mended. On arrival we spent some time in the scruffy oasis, where there was fortunately an adequate tyre shop. But the village lanes were pretty well paved with broken glass, sardine tins and old nails, and I wondered how soon it would be before Ark's next puncture. The young garage hands had their work cut out keeping the village children at bay, threatening them, though half in fun, with chisels and even pelting them with sandals every now and again as the mob drew near like clusters of infuriating flies, or sauntered by tauntingly, swaggering in their long striped gowns, and playing on ear-piercingly shrill plastic flutes. Certainly this dirty little village of modern Tudmur made a sorry contrast with the former glories of the Palmyrenes, the wonder of Zenobia, the great processions and the sacrificial rites of Ba'al. Here was only dust and dirt and heat, for the green of the true oasis lies enclosed, its palms and olives behind mud walls; the new village, sweltering outside in a garlic-scented heat is built of mud and straw plastered over stones.

A boy came up to me and said: 'Hullo, monsieur! — How many languages you speak?'

'English, Malay, a little French. How many do you speak?'

'All people's!' was the astonishingly boastful reply. Obviously the sons of Belial were flown with insolence — if not with wine.

We stayed a day and a half in Palmyra sleeping the night in the forlorn little hotel, that goes by the resounding name of 'Zenobia'. I think perhaps Palmyra was even more beautiful at night than it was in the dazzling heat of day. After dark we sat on the wall outside the hotel, and talked for some time to an Englishman who had come by bus. No baksheesh boys were allowed here and it was peaceful and very still in the moonlight looking across at the little temple of Bel Shamine that stands close to the hotel.

We spent the first afternoon in the valley of the tombs which is well away from the ruins, with an old man from the Temple of Ba'al as guide. Even more interesting than the tower tombs, were the catacombs with their neat layers of vaults that looked as if constructed only yesterday so perfectly has the desert preserved them. Many had been very recently opened. Here were reliefs of the nobles and grand ladies of Palmyra and their families, in formal groups dressed in Roman tunics and robes, reclining with their wine glasses in their hands. The family tombs are set in the wings of the vaults, others in countless shelves, layer upon layer. The whole area appears to be studded with subterranean mausoleums and—where the new *'pipe benzine'* cuts through—still more vaulted arches and solid seven-inch thick doors of stone lay freshly revealed. Many of the shelves for the dead had been cleared, and here and there modern cement bags lay crammed full of bones of long-departed Palmyrenes. Besides bas reliefs there are painted murals too; the ubiquitous eggs and bread pattern, and the wind-blown Hellenic acanthus frequently occur.

In the tombs there was a hygienic smell like that of a veterinary surgery. Outside, the desert smelt worse, for there were several carcases of long dead camels left to rot in the baking afternoon heat of this valley of the dead.

We returned past the sulphur spring of Ain Afka in which boys and men were bathing noisily, took the old man home to his Ba'al, and went back alone to the other valley. There we sat for a while, quietly and unmolestedly watching the sun set, its light turning the great temple again to that wonderful apricot-gold. Slowly, as the sun left the temples and columns, the desert background deepened in colour to a dark raspberry red flushed across with lighter bands of pink against the deep distant blue horizon.

As we drove past the Triumphal Arch the next afternoon the baksheesh boys had a final fling. One of them—whose finger-nails I noticed were painted red—even managed to weep, with frustrated rage I suppose, as we drove away into the desert, certainly never to return to be tormented by him or his kind. For a visit to Palmyra, although remarkably worth while, is I think unlikely to occur more than once in a lifetime.

❧ 16 ❧

North to Istanbul

Ark was coated red with the clinging sand of the Great Syrian
Desert, but she was running well and we were feeling remarkably
pleased with her performance. In Beirut, the Volkswagen agent
who had seen to her last servicing* said that he could not have
believed she had travelled so far on such roads, he was astounded
at her excellent mechanical condition, having seen many other
cars in a bad way after the same journey. So we were not a little
proud of her now.

As we drove back towards Homs, for the first time since Malaya,
we opened the windscreen. Driving like that was deliciously cool,
it gave one a pleasant sensation like being at sea. As we bounced
and rattled along light-heartedly Stuart decided that Ark had now
earned an honorary title—El Ark, Ship of the Desert—to be
bestowed by our sons with due ceremony on arrival in England.

We camped near the pipe-line just as the sun set into the
mountains over Homs.

It was as if the hills opened to receive the sun and swallowed it
down wolfiishly; in the east the full moon was up, the herds were
going slowly home, a few voices calling out; and far away enormous dust-devils went driving into the distance.

To prevent any vehicle running into Ark during the night, we
put a line of stones around her as we had seen the lorry drivers do,
and went to bed. When we got up in the morning the full moon
was setting over the red desert.

On this road to Homs, there were some beehive houses which
we were able to examine at leisure as they were deserted; they are
extraordinary buildings, neatly constructed with smoke holes in
the roof, said to be typical of northern Syria and, according to
Huxley, they are unique.

Kurdish dogs again dashed out to the attack, making their usual

* Her ninth—in all she was serviced eleven times, used 330 gallons of petrol
averaged 27.7 miles to the gallon, and had six punctures.

172

direct approach, judging the angle of convergence remarkably accurately even from a full two hundred yards distance. Some of them, hideously tugging out the guts of a dead donkey were too busy to give chase.

At the Homs petrol pump a man put his head in at my window, and in a friendly manner enquired : 'Tudmur* *Qwayis*?'

I had my mouth full of breakfast crispbread and spluttered back with some difficulty : 'Tudmur *Qwayis-Qwayis*!'

It certainly had been an experience which neither of us would have missed. Now, after Hama, we must make direct for the Turkish frontier if we were to have any time in Greece at all; it was already June 9th, and we were considerably behind our schedule.

That day we passed a number of the beautiful beehive villages of northern Syria; they looked extremely decorative, their delicate shades of cream, white or oatmeal standing out against the vivid background of fields—ochre, green, russet and even wine-red so dark is the soil here.

I longed frequently to stop, to admire, but Syrian village boys were a nuisance, and even the young men have a habit of rushing out from cafés blowing whistles violently, signalling one to halt and drink their unappetizing '6-down' or whatever it may be.

When we did once rashly stop to buy some eggs from a small boy on the roadside, a bigger boy raced up, pawed for baksheesh, whining and screaming. Finally he tried to prevent Ark from moving by leaning heavily against the front—much to the disgust of a young adult bystander who, although he showed his disapproval was obviously scared to interfere.

The immense and ancient wooden water wheels of Hama, continually drawing water up from the Orontes, are picturesque but we could not hear their day-long creaking for which Hama is famed, because of the Syrian drivers' extravagant use of motor horns.

In the fields farming families were busy winnowing, groups of dark figures standing in the circles of light chaff made patterns among the striped red and gold of ploughed and planted hills beyond. Ponies and donkeys drew little vehicles of saw-edged wheels round and round over the chaff, while small children rode merrily on top as if at a fair.

* The Arabic name for Palmyra.

Syrian lorries were decorated if anything even more gaily than Persian ones; plastic fruits and ridiculous plastic birds perched on green branches cluttered their windscreens.

On the whole the people seemed a cheerful lot—apart from the ferocious whistling coffee-shop youths and the angry baksheesh boys—and on the high balcony of one lorry we passed that day a row of young Arabs stood swaying in unison, hands twirling gaily, and shoulders twisting to the movements of that same Arab dance that I had learnt at the Source of Adonis.

That morning we saw the last of the desert : and turning away from it, and from the red fertile belt that skirts it we came into rocky granite hills, small trees and little tilled fields, and a part of the great Roman road that ran between Antioch and Aleppo. It is solid and splendid, paved and stone-edged : we drove Ark on it for a short distance at a point where it joins the modern road, and later saw it peter out in a fig orchard where a group of gaily dressed nomads had put up their tents.

At Bab el Hawa we crossed the frontier, where the road runs under a ruined Roman triumphal arch. Here in Turkey the change was marked : there were many green trees with oleanders flowering in their shade, rich cornfields; and the children, no longer screaming for baksheesh were actually waving, smiling, and indicating the way to Istanbul.

Here the charmingly pert little hoopoes were around again, and some neat birds, crested sandpipers, I think, and in the beautiful Rheythanli valley, where stubble was being burnt off after the harvest, was a great gathering of enormous white cranes. A high wind fanned the smoke and flames across the fields, while the crane army stood to windward on the crackling edge of the fiery stubble waiting to pounce upon escaping frogs and mice.

After skirting Antioch the road climbs steeply two thousand feet or so into the hills on the way to Iskanderum; we drew off for the night onto a small shorn field. The view was magnificent down to the White Lake, far below, and out over the wide plain beyond where the long stubble fires glowed red all night in the harvested fields under the great moon.

The next day we should see the fertile Cilician lands, from which Solomon used to buy his horses. When we awoke at four o'clock, Turkish time, the sun was already gilding the dark reddish hills across the steep valley. An hour later Belen, the mountain village in the pass to Iskanderum was already very much alive and busy, its fruit and butcher shops open, and its hot *nams* coming out of the ovens rapidly. The slender white minarets of its mosque rise up tall from a mass of little terraced and balconied houses and vine-covered verandahs above ancient aqueducts. The village crowds into and fills the pass; once through it one looks down again towards the Mediterranean, and Iskanderum with its dreamy hills pointing down to the sea and the shipping in the bay.

In Iskanderum, a pleasant clean little port, we stopped to buy bread, vodka and fruit. Iskanderum is seven hundred miles from Istanbul, so we decided then not to hurry unduly, but to camp for once at mid-day to give me a chance to catch up on some work in peace before reaching Istanbul on the Sunday—it was then Friday.

Pleasant rolling countryside led to Adana, and after Syria, it seemed very fertile. There were rows of people out hoeing in the fields, men and women alike dressed in the baggy trousers; the boys wore vivid scarlet shirts as red as the Turkish flag itself, or of that deep kingfisher blue which the Turks also love. There were storks standing on the roofs of tiny houses, busy feeding their babies in huge nests that seemed too large for the buildings that supported them. Twelfth century Armenian castles of dark stone stood in several strategic gaps in the hills, then suddenly, beyond the fields the high distant snows of the Taurus mountains reared white against the blue.

Adana—mimosa in flower, and pink and apricot-washed houses with wooden joisted upper storeys above the Seyhan river. Above Tarsus the road began climbing abruptly into the mountains. As we were finishing lunch three little boys in baggy trousers and flat caps appeared, but not to beg; we gave them sweets and cigarettes, and they taught us to say goodbye—'*Allah's marla dik*', or so it sounded. Climbing then on up towards the Cilician Gates in the footsteps of St Paul, the road follows a deep gorge, the snows high beyond. We paused at a little spring in the pine trees above a river to fill our water cans where the clear water gushed out. Here, rather oddly, we met the first prostitute we had seen for a long while : she descended from a taxi and came to wash her feet with their silver painted toe-nails at the clear spring. She had a little, tough, coarse face, and a wide friendly smile, but her silver nails, frizzed hair and rather obvious profession seemed curiously out of place in these fresh woods and hills.

Our camp of that afternoon was definitely a four-star one, but it took some little time to reach, for it was on a part of the old road, well off the new one from which we had spotted it. An idyllic place, it lay in the deep shade of a plane tree by a small sandy brook lined with firs and oleanders, above which straddled the beautiful arc of a Roman bridge overgrown with wild fig trees and pomegranates in flower. Here we settled down for a few blissful hours, spreading ourselves luxuriously, enjoying the sense of being unhurried. For once in a while we got the camp table out, and stood the fires ready in a sandy hollow under the tree, and when we had worked we began to concoct an ambitious evening stew. It was one of which we could be proud, for even corned beef tastes exotic—cooked with aubergine, raisins, pimentoes, potatoes, onions, mint, baby cucumbers, little fresh peaches, and a touch of turmeric. We ate at the table outside, and celebrated with a glass of *vin Liban*. The Turks are certainly polite, and we received no worrying visitors; once a herd of gleaming black goats came slowly up-stream, followed by a little boy who merely smiled and walked on.

Early in the morning we passed through the dramatic stone barrier of the Cilician Gates, and only too soon wished that we had lingered on in our idyllic camp-site; because, at a place called Pozanzia we were held up for three hours at a road block, due to extensive road-building operations and blasting in the high valley ahead.

We retreated from the village road-block to wait in a field by the rushing river, where a quiet young man brought glasses of clear tea from a neighbouring café, and eventually gave me a lesson in Turkish. When we did at last get into the pass, we found it filled with a wild activity—bulldozers perched precariously on rocky hillsides; Kurds and camels by the tearing river—men in rose-red shirts and black waistcoats, women in scarlet, purple and apple-green—so vivid that they looked as if they had walked out of some old-fashioned light opera.

Once over that 5,000-foot pass, the road dropped down through verdant country: the snowy tops of the Taurus standing up to the west above steep, green foothills, the valleys below thick with young poplars and mulberry trees, and the flowers were vivid.

There were fields of big flaming red poppies as dark as ox blood with a sheen among them of the tall anchusa as blue as the sky above, and wild alyssum, clumps of rose pink miniature scented campion, orange poppies, larkspur, and blue cornflowers.

Then we were tearing down to the plain below, for the first time in months at Ark's top cruising speed, dropping easily to the steppes. Although the country then became gradually less and less fertile, one sees clearly how much more fortunate is Turkey in her central plateau than Persia, with her terrible salt wastes.

The corn became poorer and thinner towards the centre of the plateau. Tuz Gölü was dead-looking, salt-caked, the salt blowing up in the wind along its eastern shores; a foxy-looking animal slunk across the road; the only pleasant thing in this bleak landscape was the little hoopoe, though he looked less assured here.

We camped at dusk by the roadside, still some 330 miles from Istanbul, and reached Ankara next day. It seemed full of tall new buildings. On its outskirts a string of racehorses was exercising early, and there were a great many of the large silver-grey 'Saluki' dogs wearing their heavy spiked anti-wolf collars. Of disturbances due to the revolution there were no signs, and we began to think that the recent *coup* must have been an extremely peaceful one.

In the hills near Bolu, rhododendrons and wild roses were in full flower, and small boys were selling little bright wild strawberries to the Sunday trippers.

At noon there was a brief but tremendous cloudburst, and some of the fine, clinging Syrian desert sand was washed off Ark at last. It was our last day in Asia and soon we were bouncing down to the Gulf of Izmit on the Sea of Marmora. Here some of the mosques looked like Christian basilicas, some like Quaker meeting halls, and now, steely-grey under cloud, the Sea of Marmora began to open out, silvery to the west, the long dark arms of land stretching before us down to the Bosphorus—the ox-ford dividing Asia from Europe.

The road began to improve and we tore along at a spanking sixty miles per hour—a high speed for Ark. We were tired but quite cheerful; we had been on the road for nearly thirteen hours, and Stuart began talking of the so memorable Chateaubriand which he and Andrew* had enjoyed the previous year in Istanbul's Park Oteli. So, weary and hungry, we began prosaically to plan

* Our younger son.

M

the wonderful dinner we would have that night, mostly because
we did not not want to think that we were about to leave Asia, the
last link with the East to which at that moment it seemed so impossible that we should ever return.

From Üsküdar there was a quick and lovely vision of the
mosques and minarets, spires and domes of Istanbul; and then we
were suddenly part of the rat race, bounding over the cobbles with
the trams and trucks and cars hurrying down on the last road in
Asia, and for us—the second ferry to cross.

We swept onto it without a pause: Leander's white tower,
delicate minarets and modern buildings swirled around briefly as
the swift ferry churned a couple of turns, and we were whisked as
hurriedly out of Asia and into Europe as if we had been caught
up willy-nilly into some mad road-race.

I looked back at the rapidly retreating Asian shore; this was
farewell Asia. I prayed silently—see you again—*Insh'a Allah!*

Stuart, who had on his previous visit, studied the roads leading
from the European side of the ferry was able to drive straight to
the Park Oteli. There we were given a delightful room, high up
above the Bosphorus, looking south across to Asia over the roofs of
Istanbul, and west to the minarets of St Sophia and the tall chim-
neys of the Seraglio above the Golden Horn.

That night we sat at a table by an open window in the dining-
room, the lights of Asia across the water, and the glitter of the
shipping in the Golden Horn. After caviare we ordered the famous
Chateaubriand, followed by fresh raspberries and cream; with
that view below it was a meal that tasted like nectar, and strangely
enough it was served by a little old waiter named Stelio, who
recognized Stuart from his previous visit, and recalled Andrew in
particular because of a capacity, remarkable in one so young, for
Chateaubriand.

Istanbul was all and more than I'd expected—an enchanting,
glamorous, gold and grey city and, although we should have been
in Athens by that date, we lingered there for three nights.

Once again it was pleasant to taste the flesh-pots, to wash the
sand out of one's hair, to have as many long hot baths as slowly
and as often as one wanted, to breakfast in our room by windows
with that so magnificent view, and to lunch and dine on fish and
kebabs, more Chateaubriand, more fresh fruit and cream.

At dusk each night we watched the Asian shore grow brilliant with a myriad points of light, and wondered when we might be able to return. But Asia, the true Asia seemed very much further away than just across the Bosphorus—it was in one sense further from here to Petra or Palmyra, or Khatmandu, than to Kuala Lumpur.

There were some interesting items on the menu; one of which —'Zephyrs de Bosphore'—tempted me, I resisted it only when Stuart asserted, though probably incorrectly, that despite its romantic-sounding name it was most likely simply 'Yesterday's whip-up'. A 'Viski-soda' was 13s. 6d. a glass, so we drank raki. At noon and at dusk, when we took our raki, the long narrow veran-dah bar outside the dining-room was crowded not only with people, but the pigeons of the Park Oteli, cooing beseechingly for their salted hazel nuts. In the cobbled streets a hundred feet below the balcony, the calls of the sellers of fruit and vegetables, of cups and cakes and of bread, came up clearly daylong, like arias in some endless opera. The voice of the muezzin too crying from his delicate minaret close to the balcony rang out at prayer times, and as we went leisurely to bed, we could see him come onto his minaret, a small dark figure against the spangled lights below, and hear him cry—'There is one God, and God is great and Muham-mad is his prophet. . . .'

There was too the water-borne sound of motor-boats on the Bosphorus, and the calls and laughter of the people who lived in the tall wooden houses and flats below, with their dogs and ducks and hens. The life of these flats became familiar : the fat woman in curlers and the blue nightdress who always sat at her window; the pretty red-haired girl who leant out above her flower-boxes; the small unattended child in bright socks who balanced pre-cariously on his scooter on a high balcony; the people who let down baskets each day to the man who sold vegetables from the panniers of a horse decorated with turquoise beads; and above all there was the endless whirring—the tearing silk sound of pigeons' wings.

There is a limit to sight-seeing and endless mosques can be a weariness to the flesh, we undertook only a little gentle exploring of Istanbul, by taxi, while Ark was being serviced. There is too much to see in Istanbul in a short time, but the memories I have are vivid. Among the clearest is the courtyard of the beautiful Suleiman Mosque, its busy but peaceful atmosphere of a well-used place of prayer, not a show place, so very different from the feeling in St Sophia : people passing in and out, tough-looking soldiers walking in pairs hand in hand; its fountains; its pigeons, and its nests of kittens, fed by charity, and guarded by a smiling young cripple. The hot *souks* nearby—also full of pigeons and loud with a tremendous roar of human voices like one vast party; and beyond—the streets of gold, of spices, of Arab silks, and the great gloomy St Sophia ruined, to my mind, by Islamic additions of prayer 'play-pens', and huge painted medallions hung below the vast dome; the famous Seraglio and its gorgeous china collection; the ancient Hippodrome with its so astoundingly perfect Egyptian obelisk. The lively Sultan Ahmat Mosque with its majestic and truly colossal pillars, its stalactite cupolas, its six minarets, and—outlandish touch of home—a seventeenth century grandfather clock from London. The rush of people and traffic on the Galatea Bridge, the thousands upon thousands of pigeons on the steps of the grey mosque there at the corner; the vast and busy market; the extraordinary effect of the radiating lines of arches in the underground cisterns of the 'palace that has sunk'. . . .

But I think what I enjoyed most of all in Istanbul was the view of the Bosphorus from our wide windows, with that foreground of animated operatic life in the steep car-free maze of cobbled streets below, and the lights of Asia across the way, a promise—or a query—for the future.

Home into Europe

On our last morning in Istanbul we stocked in fresh supplies from the little delicatessen shops across the road. Black olives, and liver sausage, Turkish cheeses, twisted crisp golden brown bread, some peculiar-looking waxed caviare, and huge red cherries so pointed that their gleaming succulent globes recalled the domes of Istanbul itself.

We had posted our final letters, we had bought the latest English and American newspapers; Ark was packed, ready waiting on the steep drive. We ought to go, but still we lingered—we both wanted once again to see the Asian shore. So we returned for a raki, and a last look over the Bosphorus from that balcony. As usual, the hotel pigeons were waiting, greedy for their midday nuts; and the voices of the street vendors rang up from below, the endless background chorus to the life of Istanbul.

When we did eventually drag ourselves away a procession of students was going down the hill carrying banners and flags. It was an orderly march in protest against the fate of fellow students who had died under the old régime during the riots of the previous month.*

We crossed over the Galatea Bridge and passed the grey mosque on the corner where mobs of pigeons still clustered on the steps as if for ever waiting for the doors to open at prayer time. And so up the hill, under Valerian's aqueduct, towards the Hadrian Gate.

The drive to the Greek border was rather an uneventful one, through a flat, military zone : soldiers everywhere, the sentries standing in gay pink and white striped band boxes, like something out of musical comedy.

That afternoon we crossed our twenty-fifth frontier into Greece, the eleventh land of the journey, and began the long run down to Athens.

Now there were fields of splendid wheat; and magnificent cattle, rather to our surprise—water buffaloes, the first since India; and of course pigs, also the first since India, the last non-Muslim

---

* It was *said* that their bodies had been put on ice, and later sold as horse flesh.

country. The people were fair-haired and friendly looking; smiling boys and girls waved and called out in greeting as we passed, and the women, so refreshingly independent in bearing, strolled along, smiling and laughing, spinning as they went. It was pleasant to be in a Christian country again at long last, and to see the freedom that Christianity gives to women so clearly expressed in their faces.

Beyond the Strimon Bridge—on the second night—we camped peacefully by the sea below dark Mount Athos, and the next day drove on in rain through a green countryside of great plane trees and holm oaks.

Towards mid-day the weather improved, though Olympus stood dark and angry, her head lost in rain clouds. It was lonely here in the mountains but increasingly beautiful. We stopped for lunch in the Vale of Tempe, where the River Peneus runs between Olympus and Ossa.

It was a long drive over the plains of Thessaly. Towards Lamia the road began to climb up into the hills, we stopped in a tiny village to buy hot mutton and *retsina*. Then up over the pass of Thermopylai feeling exhilarated now—it was always the same we found in each new country. The new atmosphere and new beauty excited us and made us gay; although progress was slow because Ark was now groaning agonizingly on every bend however carefully she was driven, and both the front mud-guards were practically scraping the tyres..

We camped late somewhere in the high mountains, and Stuart started driving early the next morning while it was still dark and I was still half asleep in the back. We stopped to brew tea near a place called of all things—Petra, and drove on through well cultivated fields and so down again towards the dark blue sea, and came into Athens early.

Those northern Greek roads had been the final straw. The Volkswagen garage people took a quick look at Ark, and said not only had the torsion bars gone but also the shock-absorbers, and as it was now Saturday—as usual it was the weekend—nothing could be done. So we made a booking for the Monday morning, picked up our letters, and went to lunch at a little place south of Athens on the coast, on whitebait, baby octopuses and *retsina,* and so out to Poseidon at Sounion.

That evening we chose a bay about forty miles from Athens,

not far from Sounion. The rocky headland that divided the bay
was grown over with stunted firs and bushes encircling a little
dancing floor for goats—or for Pan perhaps—high above the sea,
and the small narrow neck of land that linked it to the foreshore
was ideal for Ark. There we camped for two blissful nights, even if
Sunday trippers were to come we felt that the position was
almost impregnable, like a Crusader castle we were defended on
almost all sides. In front, below a little cliff lay the clear sea in the
angle of the headland; behind, the narrow col fell away sharply to
the other arm of the bay, and beside us rose the dancing floor. We
bathed in the tiny cove below, the water was cold but we soon
warmed up while cooking the supper and settling in. The picnickers had gone, the bay was ours for the night, some distance
away the road circled round a back-drop of hills, there was the
sound of goat bells as the herds went home up almost vertical hillsides. The pattern of this pastoral life seemed always with us, and
we were very much at home among it now.

The next morning we set about cleaning out Ark thoroughly,
for the third and last time on the trek, and on this occasion it was
for England that we were preparing. We removed most, though by
no means all, of the desert sands from the various cupboards and
crannies, re-sorted the stores, now a sadly meagre collection only,
the journey being nearly done, and while Stuart cleaned the cooking fires and lamps, I washed our clothes, and in a final spate of
energy even went as far as to wash down the floor. Our labours
done we sat back, gratifyingly houseproud and only wishing that
we had some good friends coming to supper that evening.

During Sunday a few parties of Greek picnickers came out from
Athens and settled on the long twin beaches on either side of our
col, bathing, fishing, and basking in the sun. But before evening
they packed up and went home and we were alone again on our
Pan headland above the sea; the stars came out, some lighted ships
passed by, and we spent another quiet happy evening.

At half-past four in the morning a white ship sailed across the
mouth of the bay, her lighted portholes as brilliant as fire-flies in
the half-light. Then, closer inshore a string of fishing boats
chugged slowly by, their small lights pinpoints in the grey-blue
early morning sea. The last sliver of the waning moon hung serene
in the clear dawn sky—the moon which we had seen full over
Palmyra.

As we moved off the grassy col and away from the wide arms of the empty bay the sound of goat bells rang clearly across the brightening sea; the first herd coming tempestuously down the steep hill above.

The day in Athens was a crowded and a tiring one, and at the end of it, we were forced to press on for we could not afford to stay the night in an Athenian hotel.

We made our pilgrimage to the Acropolis. After the golden and apricot-coloured stones of the Hellenic Middle East, the Parthenon seemed intensely pure and white, beautifully simple in the morning sunlight above the dreaming, hazy city spread below. After some hours there we descended to the Grand Bretagne to read yesterday's English Sunday papers, to write picture postcards like good tourists, to sip iced drinks and watch the crowds in their gay summer dresses, and in fact to gape at our first European city. We had come, so to speak, the reverse way from the usual one, both in time and space; we had seen first the far outposts of the Hellenic influence and of the Roman Empire, and now were drawing in almost too abruptly to the focal points of European civilization.

While I looked with interest at the chimney-pot hats which the women wore that summer, civilization began to affect us both —Stuart almost to bravado. His curly hair was touselled, his eyes seemed more tip-tilted than usual, his tongue sharper; he could only make caustic remarks about the new hats, the wealthy tourists; and nibble at bits of sesame halo bread that he produced casually from his pockets under the horrified eyes of sleek young waiters in the elegant new bar of the Grand Bretagne.

I thought it was time that we moved on; 'snobisme du desert' can be carried too far.

When Ark was ready for the road again at six o'clock, we left Athens, or tried to leave. We took a short cut, and perhaps owing to tiredness—the day had begun at four—we lost ourselves for the first time since that rainy morning in Persia. In such a small and civilized city as Athens it was ridiculous: furious with ourselves we went wearily round in circles in the slums of Piraeus. We emerged at last on the Sacred Way, where we should have been nearly an hour ago, and from it saw again the glory of the Acropolis gleaming in the sunset above the city.

At Daphni we were sorely tempted to take refuge in the

'Tourist Pavilion'—being lost in the slums of Athens for an hour
had exhausted us more than anything else so far, but we resisted
the temptation, fortified ourselves with Greek brandy, and acquired half a dozen large fresh eggs, with the aid of a kindly man
who ran to buy them from a house in the monastery garden.

Then the sun set in a red-gold west over the sea, and the sight
of it, and the fresh breeze blowing in our faces from across the dark
waters of the Bay of Salamis revived us still further. We pushed
remorselessly on again, to camp at dusk in a spacious olive grove,
where we ate a great many hot boiled eggs and sesame halo bread,
and were soon asleep.

Through flowery Thebes we drove into the hills—beehives and
goat bells, and the hot scent of flowers and wild thyme—and to
Delphi under the slopes of towering Parnassus, as millions of
pilgrims had done for centuries before us.

Despite the tourists Delphi is still impressive, enigmatically
dreaming in the sun on its steep shoulder of Parnassus, above the
acres of olive groves, and the jewel blue of the sea, far below. In
something of the same way as El Khazneh, Delphi seems to be
guarding a secret, a more savage and archaic one than the
Khazneh's, closer in feeling perhaps to the Source of Adonis.

We ate on one of the wooden platform-like balconies that jut
out from the village street, perched on stilts high above the hillside
which reminded me of those of Damascus' El Ghouta. One felt
as if one were seated in mid-air above the deep sun-filled ravine of
Pleistos below. Rough rosy-ochre coloured fields fell abruptly
away to the seas of olives and the blue curve of the Bay of Itea on
the Gulf of Corinth where the pilgrims used to land.

It was now hot on the hillside; and the pure white beauty of the
mysterious little tholus, built in the fifth century B.C., drew us
irresistibly off the road and away from the people. So we
scrambled down and spent a peaceful afternoon in the shade of
the olives, looking down upon the perfection of the white marble
pillars that stood out against the heat-hazed blue of the hills
opposite—lazing, and dreaming and painting. This was the atmosphere of Delphi, pagan, quiet, almost benignly antique, here one
could lose all sense of time.

No one came our way, and it was so peaceful that Stuart slept
a little, lying in the shade beside me. Then as the sun began to drop
behind Parnassus, we went up to the Sanctuary, following the

Sacred Way past the Castalia, the spring in the cleft in which the pilgrims used to bathe, below cliffs that the Nabataeans themselves would have enjoyed carving.

We spent the night in Ark under the great cliffs of the Castalia and in the morning set off for Egoumenitea, where we hoped to catch our third ferry—to Corfu—on the following day. The land was beautiful, as if overflowing with natural riches : sweet corn, olives, figs, vines, oranges, wild clematis, soft tufted golden bundles of newly-harvested wheat. We stopped to buy large strawberries, apricots and green figs.

At eight o'clock we camped in an olive grove that was loud with the song of bull frogs. I was chopping up vegetables for the evening stew with Ark's dagger-like kitchen knife, when a boy of about fifteen looked in and passed the time of day, presently a little chap of eight or nine joined him. The older boy indicated that I might as well chop off the little fellow's head—a tremendous joke which they both enjoyed. When we had given them some sweets and let the small boy play with 'Ararat' they presently departed cheerfully into the dusk.

We were still one hundred and fifty miles from Egoumenitea and the road was then in bad condition. At the Louros River we stopped to wash our feet, this branching river was clear and fast-flowing over white stones under the full green foliage of numerous dark-stemmed plane trees growing with their roots in the water.

It was late in the afternoon when we at last reached the ferry town. The Bank was closed, but someone very obligingly reopened it as we needed to cash more travellers' cheques. The ferry was a small 'Ship Landing Tank'. We ate our supper on board, then I fell fast asleep in Ark and did not waken until we arrived some four hours later in Corfu. There we drove off into the darkness, dazed and sleepy and without the slightest idea where to go. By chance we ended up in a *cul-de-sac* on a hill top; it was pitch dark, we did not know where it was, and we were too exhausted to bother. We drank a glass of Samos wine from Thebes, and, thus cheered, crawled into our sleeping bags.

Morning light revealed a little canopied carriage arriving with neat tourists at the trim white 'Tourist Pavilion' at Kanino, above Ulysses Isle. Had we known, we could have gone to bed at least washed and clean, now we crept up the steps to the 'pavilion' feeling rather like a couple of bedraggled Bedouin.

Eventually we found our way through lanes hedged with myrtle across the island to a Homeric bay, where we lazed away two days and two nights in an olive grove by the sea.

The mistral dropped, and I lay outside on one of the camp beds and read, until a charming Greek-American artist, who was camped nearby, come over and began to talk.

He had an attractive French wife and a handsome little boy of four, whom we entertained in Ark with the help of 'Ararat'—whose voice was now just about on cracking point.

It was a most restful, peaceful place, with its tiny *langouste* restaurant, its white doves in the olive groves, a little boy selling fresh green figs kept clean under their own leaves, and a smiling old woman who strolled around with her spinning, keeping an eye on the girl sand workers who came by sea, and sometimes rebuking any young man who gazed overlong at any particular girl—but it was almost too like a picture postcard, and I felt no inclination to paint.

On the Monday morning we recrossed the island to the town and, formalities gaily completed with the shipping people over a glass of wine, we drove to the harbour. There we got a shock on seeing the ferry, it had a drive-on entrance big enough only for saloon cars. Presently we learnt that the shipping people had arranged for Ark to be lifted on board, but this was still worse, for the derrick looked both dilapidated and inadequate. We drove alongside with sinking hearts: slings were lowered, and a great deal of shouting and heated argument ensued. Presently a man asked how much Ark weighed. We were not exactly sure—a little under two tons—we were more anxious to know what load their derrick could lift: eventually they announced that it was a two-tonner. Then, among a fresh spate of yells and fulminating commands Ark was hoisted painful inch by inch.

At this crucial moment Stuart was called away to sign some papers, and I was left alone to watch, with butterflies in my stomach. The gear was far from new, and I expected to see Ark drop back at any moment with a ghastly crash squashed on the quayside. But she was swung inboard safely, and we spent a long lazy day on deck crossing the Adriatic.

Brindisi was unexpectedly attractive, and soon we were tearing across Italy. We had done 11,300 miles, and the race to the Channel was now on.

The Appian Way led us over the hills, through some superbly lovely ancient villages crowded on sharp crests. War memories at Salerno; and the most succulent peaches we had had for years, eaten blatantly by the sea under little dumpy palms, both of us unashamedly dripping small pools of peach juice on to the promenade. Then the gay, flamboyant road to Amalfi, under Dantesque cliffs and dark storm clouds; and crowded, trippery, glittering Amalifi itself. We hurried on, a little appalled, to find a quiet hotel in Santa Agata sui due Golfo at the end of the peninsula. The next day was my birthday; a civilized meal overlooking the Bay of Naples, and as many baths as I wanted were to be part of Stuart's birthday gifts.

We watched the clouds blowing off the craggy hill tops, and on them the lights coming out as high as stars in the sky, and glittering too under Vesuvius in Naples across the bay. We dined on our balcony high above the vines, a smiling maid and a friendly young waiter brought iced champagne and a simple but delicious meal. Perhaps best of all, however, were the hot baths, the first for twelve days—since Istanbul.

But we had to push on again: the next day—Pompeii, and crowds of tourists and touts: Herculaneum—lovely and almost empty in the later afternoon.

In Rome we had only a few hours. We left Ark under the walls of the Colosseum; dwarfed there, and travel-stained, she now showed honourable scars—paint scorched off the roof box on the port side, and tattered remains of Lebanese election posters clinging irremovably with gum and Syrian sand. After lunch we took an open carriage to the Fontana di Trevi and duly threw in our coins, and then a brief visit to St Peter's rather shook our Islamically-attuned minds. It happened to be St Peter's Day; the interior was hung with red banners; there were massed banks of brilliant flowers, and many lighted tapers and candles twinkling. St Peter with his black face, and his toe kissed almost flat, sitting among the glitter inevitably brought to mind familiar God of Hell images smothered in opium dregs in spangled, incense-laden Chinese temples. Gaudy St Peter's was a far cry from the dignified austerity of mosques such as that of El Aksa at Jerusalem.

Sienna, dreaming and golden; a high camp on the pass above Florence; and then the great autostradas bore Ark swiftly with the tide northwards.

On the eve of our twenty-second wedding anniversary we found ourselves almost running out of Italy; not wanting a chilly camp high on the Simplon road, we paused for a swim in the lake at Baveno, and dinner in an hotel there. We could not afford to sleep in the hotel and having looked with increasing horror at the 'camping-camping lidos', we felt unable to face them. So after dinner, served overlooking the darkening lake, we crept away to a marble dump which we had already noted, such as one would hardly have expected to find on the crowded shores of Maggiore; on the very edge of the lake it was secluded under willows among marble blocks and chippings.

After Greece and the Middle East, Italy seemed unbelievably overcrowded. We had almost forgotten too how small Switzerland was, and the roads were so good that we all but ran through the country without the pause we had intended having there. But we deliberately lingered one afternoon resting and sun-bathing by Lake Yverdon, and camped later in the Jura, in a disused quarry grown over with wild flowers and strawberries, not far from the French border.

Now there was only one more country to cross, and one more ferry to catch. France was wet and cold, and the grey Nordic shades began to close down depressingly.

But at midday the sun came out and we were cheered as we lunched in a clover field, off Rochefort and red wine, and above our heads the larks were singing. Perhaps it was not going to be so hard to live in the North after all.

The next day in deluging rain, we parked Ark with some pride in the heart of Paris, in the Champs Elysées itself, and went off to arrange for the channel passage, collect our letters, and find an hotel for the night.

The thread was drawn out; the trek was over. Now we wanted only to get home, and to see the family. More easily than we had expected we were able to book a Channel passage, so we left Paris the next day—and for the last time the P.W.D. provided our pull-in for the night, a disused road off the highway to Calais.

The morning was one of light rain and intermittent sunshine. Then the Channel lay below, capped with countless white horses. And our fifth and last ferry took us home to England—and the start of a new life.

INDEX